WOW Woman of Worth

15 Empowered Entrepreneurs
Share Success Stories with Soul

Christine Awram

Published by Inspire Higher Consulting Inc. February, 2018
ISBN: 9781775094920

Editor: Danielle Anderson
Typeset: Greg Salisbury
Book Cover Design: Judith Mazari - www.judithmazari.net

DISCLAIMER: Readers of this publication agree that neither Christine Awram, nor her publisher will be held responsible or liable for damages that may be alleged as resulting directly or indirectly from the use of this publication. Neither the publisher nor the author can be held accountable for the information provided by, or actions, resulting from, accessing these resources.

This book is dedicated to my grandmother, Emily Louise Adkin, who lived past her 100th birthday with all faculties intact.

This courageous woman raised five children on her own during the Great Depression after leaving her abusive husband. She consistently demonstrated strength and determination while maintaining a remarkable sense of humour.

She was also a deeply compassionate woman. "Nanny" was my safe harbour, especially when I was a little girl and my world felt so very scary. The most powerful childhood memory I have is when I would curl up on her lap in her rocking chair, and she would endlessly stroke my hair while rocking my fears away. Never have I felt so completely cherished and safe.

She exemplified every trait of a Woman Of Worth. She inspired me to keep my heart open, even in the darkest hours. I still miss you Nanny, and I will love you forever.

The WOW Credo

I am a Woman Of Worth
My worthiness is inherent and infinite –
    it is my natural state
My value is a reflection of who I AM –
    and I am magnificent
Who I am always makes a difference –
    because I MATTER
I am successful –
    coming from my true power which lies within
I am empowered –
    making choices from the clarity of my heart, mind and
    spirit
I am an empowered leader –
    impacting others from quiet acts of kindness to
    leading a nation
I am abundant –
    manifesting success from my core values
I cherish my relationships –
    they are part of what makes me strong
I am a Human BEing –
    as my BEing is of far more significance than my
    DOing
I play, laugh, and bring beauty and light into the world –
    I am RADIANT
At times I despair and I weep –
    when I feel the pain of a world that has momentarily
    gone mad
Yet even when I tremble through a dark night of the soul,
    I renew my faith and my courage in a single heartbeat
    because my spirit is indomitable
I feel, and I care, and I am passionately alive –
    with a heart as open as the universe

I AM A WOMAN OF WORTH, AND I AM GLORIOUS

Acknowledgements

This entire book could be filled with the names of all the people I want to thank, for the many ways you've all helped inspire this book to become a reality. Heartfelt gratitude to the tremendous community I call my WOW Tribe. You rock.

To the fifteen fabulous females who are this book's contributing authors, you have staggered me with your willingness to show up 100%. Each and every one of you share my burning desire to make our world a more joyful and empowered place, and you've been the most courageous and extraordinary women to collaborate with. It has been an honour.

To my publisher Julie Salisbury, for taking my hand every step of the way while sharing your brilliance and making this adventure fun. You shine a very bright light my friend.

To my family and closest friends, you are the inner circle of my Tribe. I have no words to express how grateful I am for your love, and that you always have my back.

And especially to David Samuelson, my beloved Manly Man. You always believe in me, and see the best in me. I couldn't have done this without your love, faith and support. You are my heart.

Contents

Introduction

You are not alone.

Successful women are rarely born that way. Almost every empowered CEO, manager, entrepreneur, and "motherpreneur" I've known has come from humble beginnings and, sometimes, almost unspeakable pain and suffering.

The reason they thrive is not because success was handed to them. Instead, these women flourish because they embraced courage and connection. At some point they made a decision to not allow their past to define them, but rather to strengthen and empower them.

Courage isn't an absence of fear – it's feeling the fear and stepping forward anyway. Life might bring you to your knees, but you don't have to stay there. Empowered women know that when you bond with like-minded women, there will always be someone to extend a hand to help you back up. We're not meant to do it alone. Together, we're stronger.

This book is a collection of real-life stories from fifteen fabulous females who have moved through extraordinary challenges to have successful and joyful lives. So often when we feel stuck or overwhelmed, when we believe we aren't good enough, when we're in pain and on our knees in the dark, it truly seems like there's no way out.

These influential women have bared it all, sharing their profoundly personal stories so you know there is always a way forward. Not only that, you'll see what a powerful place this is to lead from.

As Goethe quoted, "Whatever you can do, or dream you can do, begin it. Boldness has genius, power, and magic in it. Begin it now." If I could add one more line specific to women it would be, "Find your Tribe, because real women empower women."

Everyone has a dream, a vision, a hope, a desire. What step forward are you willing to take today? Connect, collaborate, take that step, and before you know it you'll be flying. This is your time darling. Get WOWed.

1

THE HOW OF WOW TO NOW

by Christine Awram, Founder
Woman Of Worth WOW Worldwide

"Great women empower other women to be great."
Christine Awram

The How of WOW to Now

By Christine Awram, Founder
Woman Of Worth WOW Worldwide

"It's time to open your eyes and get started."

I jolted awake and jumped out of bed, head whirling. What? Wait! What? I'd just had the wildest dream, but it wasn't exactly a dream. I thought I was awake. Did I drift off? What just happened?

I'd been having a chat with…a light. A light with a voice. Believe me, I know how crazy it sounds.

It was early 2004, and I was being instructed by some woo-woo light-voice to create an empowerment event called WOW Woman Of Worth in May – which was only weeks away – at a golf and country club, with celebrity speaker Linda Edgecombe as the headliner. I was to create a powerful day with world-class speakers, philanthropy, connection, education, and collaboration, where women would celebrate their magnificence.

That's when I woke up. I'd had some weirdo metaphysical experiences in my life, but this was taking it to a whole new level.

I didn't know much about producing events, but I knew enough to know that pulling together an event of this magnitude in less than three months was ridiculous.

Or was it?

I pondered my options. This "vision" (for lack of a better word) had been strangely compelling. Most of my life had been spent struggling with a lack of self-worth, and I knew I wasn't the only one. While I had always wanted to make a difference and see more women embrace their fabulousness, this wasn't how I thought it would play out.

But why not?

I decided that the only thing to do was put it to the test. I'd been "told" the date and venue, so I called the country club and said I needed their event space. She exclaimed, "You're in luck! We just had a cancellation for that date a few minutes ago, so the space is available. Normally you'd have to book at least a year in advance."

Whoa.

I was a bit freaked out. Now what? A second test of course! I'd also been "told" that Linda Edgecombe, who was one of Canada's top speakers, would be the headliner. She was in high demand, and I barely knew her. This would have to be the acid test.

I looked up her office number and called, fully expecting voicemail or a receptionist. The phone was picked up and I heard a chirpy voice declaring, "Hi, this is Linda."

Seriously? I mean really, could this get any stranger?

"Linda!" I chirped back. "It's Christine Awram. You probably won't remember me; we met at that aromatherapy workshop a while back."

"Christine! Of course I remember you. What's up?"

I took a deep breath and plunged in.

"I had this idea. I'd like to produce an annual empowerment event for women called WOW Woman Of Worth, and I want to launch the first one in May. Most events are either all professional or all personal, and I'd like to create a new type of event that weaves them both together. It would be nine to five with lunch included, and I'll bring in some great speakers on different topics where women want answers. You'll be the headliner, we'll have entertainment, and the main focus would be on getting women to really celebrate how magnificent they are."

A pause. "Sounds great but…I get booked as much as two years in advance, and that's only a couple months away."

"I know it's a long shot but, well, I had this really vivid dream, and in my dream you were the headliner. I know it's a little crazy, but I decided to just call and lay it on you."

"Fair enough. What kind of speaker fee did you have in mind?"

"Um, actually no speaker fee, as you'd get some great exposure and most of the event's proceeds would support a local women's charity."

There was a lengthy pause. "Hang on a sec." She put me on hold. As I waited, it seemed certain I'd stepped way over the line and would be on hold for the rest of my natural life.

Then Linda was back.

"This is the strangest thing," she began. "When my assistant is out doing errands, I let the phone go to voicemail. She was out, the phone rang, and I literally heard a voice telling me to answer the phone. I did, and there you were asking me to headline an event that's never been done, on a date that's only weeks away, and with no speaker fee. Part of me is thinking wow, this chick has balls, but another part is saying hey, remember the freaky voice telling you to answer the phone! When my assistant came back in, I put you on hold and asked her what's happening on that date. You're not going to believe what she told me."

"I bet she said you've had a cancellation on that date." Yet another momentous pause.

"Not only did I have a cancellation, it was just made this morning."

"So, are you in?"

She started to laugh. I joined right in, and the two of us howled like loons. It was one of those magical moments that can never be planned or anticipated.

"I'm in. It makes no sense, I don't know why I'm saying yes, but there's something going on that I don't understand yet and need to be a part of."

That was fourteen years ago. Linda has been an integral part of WOW every single year, along with some of the most powerful speakers in the world. We have grown to empower over 10,000 women firsthand, rescue our global sisters from slavery, support philanthropic projects locally, and now publish #1 bestselling books that donate 100% of royalties to charity. It has turned into a community of extraordinary women that I call "Tribe," where great women empower other women to be great.

There are three key takeaways that I want to leave you with:

Trust Your Gut

I saw a quote the other day that said, *"Told you so. Sincerely, Your Intuition."*

Intuition is the place where you are hard-wired to your soul. It bypasses the logical left hemisphere of your brain and hits you right in the gut. Never discount it.

Pay attention. Make a decision, take an action step, and see where it leads. Always give yourself permission to audaciously ask, because the worst that can happen is they'll say no. Remember that the world is full of flat squirrels who couldn't decide what to do.

Know Your Why

If you are being called to start a business, create an event, take a sabbatical, write a book, or whatever is pulling at you, it's critical to understand your "Why." What is the underlying purpose of your calling that's specific and personal to YOU.

If you read our first WOW book where I shared my story, I related the core of my "Why": the time I was beaten on a public street in broad daylight at the age of nine. No one intervened, and all I remember thinking was, "I'm not even worth saving." This led to a lifetime of believing I was inherently worthless.

Fast forward to Woman Of Worth. Coincidence? Absolutely not. I wasn't consciously aware of my underlying purpose when I had the vision, but it became crystal clear in very short order.

Build A Tribe

I've had many dark nights of the soul. If there's a mistake to be made, I've made it. At times I've been on my knees in despair, not knowing how I can possibly go on. Then I remember I'm not alone, and call on my Tribe.

Together, we're stronger.

What does Tribe look like? One example is when my mom had a massive stroke, and I was having a hard time staying on top of business for the six weeks she was in hospital. Then she died, and I was almost immobilized. I reached out to my inner circle and they joined together to make sure things got done, no questions asked.

Another example is when one of my best friends suddenly died from pancreatic cancer. The tribe banded together to create a fundraising memorial, because she was a single mom of a seven-year-old son. In less than a month we created a magnificent send off and raised over $50,000 to go into trust for her child.

Tribe has got your back. It's about collaboration, not competition. You share values and rarely judge. There's no bitchiness or jealousy.

When you need to vent, your Tribe brings the wine and listens. They never let you stay in your shit, though, because after you've vented, the next questions are, "Are you done? Is there more? Then it's time to move on. What can you learn from this? What's next?" This lights the way to creative solutions and healing.

How "Tribe" and This Book are Powerfully Linked

This is the second WOW book in a series, which was inspired by "Chicken Soup for the Soul." I loved the concept of different authors sharing their authentic stories, and especially how life events can bring about empowerment instead of victimhood.

So often we observe amazing women and believe we can never do what they've done. There can be a tendency to think, "I'm not as smart, I don't have the resources, I'm not qualified, I need to take another course, I can't follow my dream until the kids are older, these women had a better education or more money."

Blah, blah, blah.

All our authors have had challenges, and some of them have experienced unspeakable pain. The common thread that runs through all their stories is that somewhere along the way, they made a decision to learn and heal from their challenges and to collaborate with others so they could move forward.

The focus for this particular book is that every single woman is an empowered entrepreneur, and she's sharing her story to inspire you and show you how it can be done. It's real and relatable, so you get to clearly see how it's possible to move forward toward your own personal dream.

In Closing

When you trust your gut, know your "Why" and understand how profoundly you matter, you attract exactly the right people into your inner circle. The common denominator is you're all aligned and authentic, and that you understand the magical power of collaboration. We're not meant to do it alone.

I will share again the final passage from my chapter in the first book, because it is a mantra that we all need to accept into our lives.

Your true sense of worth is never externally sourced. It doesn't come from your spouse, house, bank account, job title, or those fabulous Jimmy Choo shoes. The real strength and power of your worth comes from within, and it's simply humbling in its magnitude.

Take time every day to heighten your awareness of who you are, why you're here, and how deeply you matter. Make the decision to give your life the meaning you CHOOSE to give it. You're the director, the producer, the star. When you identify with the glorious Woman Of Worth that you truly are, you empower everyone and your worthiness can never be taken from you.

About Christine Awram

"Chocolate is a vegetable, because it comes from a bean." This is just one of many doubletake statements you'll hear from Christine Awram (while wearing a pink tiara), as she encourages women to question any of their beliefs that limit an empowered, joyful, and successful life.

She's the founder of Woman Of Worth WOW Worldwide and is a dynamic speaker, author, visionary, and philanthropist. Christine radiates vitality with her indomitable spirit and humour. Yet her earlier years began as a teenage runaway who experienced addiction, illness and depression. She inspires others by sharing the specific strategies she used to move from futility to fulfillment, and how she transformed challenges into passion and purpose.

Christine's commitment to the empowered leadership of women resulted in her being honoured with the Outstanding Leadership Award by the Global Women's Summit. She has personally inspired over 10,000 women through her WOW events, and believes she is just getting warmed up.

www.aWomanOfWorth.com
www.theWOWevent.com
Facebook: aWomanOfWorthWOW
LinkedIn: wowchristineawram
Twitter: @womanofworthwow

2

"WHY ME" TO "WHAT FOR"

by Crystal Flaman

*"Somewhere inside all of us is the power
to change the world."*
Roald Dahl

"Why Me" to "What For"

By Crystal Flaman

We've all had a few "defining moments" in our lives where something happened, or didn't happen, that altered the course of our lives forever. Some defining moments are absolutely fabulous! Crossing paths with a stranger who becomes a lifelong friend. Meeting the love of your life when you least expect it. Having someone tell you that they believe in you and because of that, you believed in yourself and went on to do extraordinary things that were so highly unlikely they bordered on impossible. These moments leave us inspired, empowered, and confident of our future path. Yes, these are the moments we love and that define us in immeasurable ways.

Then there's the other, less-invited kind of defining moment that blindsides us when we least expect it. They throw us off course and cause us to seriously question our direction and purpose in life. They happen when we're busy making other plans. Illness. Divorce. Starting a business and being so financially stretched that finding a few pennies makes you feel rich. Freak accident where bones are crushed and dreams are shattered.

I know defining moments happen in all of our lives, because all of these moments have happened to me. As a woman navigating through life for over forty-five years, and as an entrepreneur of more than twenty years, I'd like to share with you three simple strategies that have helped me maneuver through some of the more challenging moments in my life. I've learned that it's imperative to intentionally create meaning from those crucial moments that so easily could have defined me.

Find a Bigger Problem Than Your Own Personal Problems or Your Own Bottom Line

One year ago, I broke my foot. I was mid-step when a 200-pound box fell on the back of my right lower leg, hitting my calf muscle and raised heel, crushing my foot into the ground, shattering the first metatarsal joint above the arch of my foot – the most important joint for walking and running – along with severely damaging the big toe joint and spraining the toe. It was one of those freak accidents you hope never happens to you. One moment I was standing there with huge aspirations of running forever, or at least until my mid nineties, and the next moment I found myself crawling out from under the box. The pain in my foot was nauseating, but the fear of not being able to run was even more excruciating.

I am a runner. A long-distance runner. For thirty years, moving physically has been an integral part of almost every day simply because it brings me joy. I also use this gift to raise funds, a lot of funds, for charity. I had several future races planned before the accident and was about to sign up for my next one. The possibility of never being able to run again or being immobile for even a short period of time caused more anxiety than I could fathom.

The break was bad, and the prognosis was bleak. ER. X-rays. CT scans. A meeting with the surgeon who advised me to take a leave from work for six months and dismissed my response when I tried to explain that I was self-employed and needed to work. Surgery took place a week later, and the throbbing pain in my foot continued to gnaw away at my usual good mood. Metal staples. Crutches. A knee scooter for months. As my doctor took the staples out, she read the surgeon's report and said, "You will walk with a limp and never run again. You're just going to have to deal with it and accept your new reality." With that, she removed the last staple and walked out.

I remained in her tiny office, a crying, hysterical mess. The stress of her words caused half of my hair to fall out, and I fell into a dark despair for those first few months. Reality was grim. No driving or walking for three to four months. *No running! How will I survive*, I wondered. The indefinite and irreparable damage was evident, not just to my foot but to my spirit. Months of rehab ensued, with thousands of dollars spent in a desperate attempt to hold on to my dream of running long distances once again. I tried everything: physiotherapy, acupuncture, shock wave therapy, reflexology, massage, hypnotherapy, alternative healing modalities, herb poultices, and countless other remedies. I cried myself to sleep for days that turned into weeks that turned into months. I was devastated, not just because my foot was broken but because running was my life, and my life as I knew it was over!

Time passed. Months passed. A year passed. And as much as I thought I would, I didn't die.

Time may never completely heal physical or emotional injuries, but what it provided me with was a space to begin to create a "bigger problem" than my own personal dilemma. The passing of time can do that for all of us. It can allow an opportunity for us to pause and then create something new, different, and possibly even better than we originally had planned. It sounds so cliché but we can create a new trajectory of our life, even more magnificent than the one we were on, by simply asking ourselves, *"What can I learn from this?"* In doing so, we move from dwelling on and magnifying our own problems (why me?) to a place of meaning and purpose (what for?).

It took time, patience, and a lot of cursing, but two things helped me navigate the reality of my broken foot and broken spirit, moving through one of the greatest valleys of my life to a time of tremendous growth and inspiration. I hope these ideas will help you, too.

1. Do something of value with your time.

I don't believe that things happen for a "reason." I believe that when unfortunate things happen in our lives, we can intentionally create meaning from those moments and, in doing so, force ourselves from a state of suffering to a place where we are learning something new, doing something differently, and becoming incredibly resilient in the process. After the initial shock of breaking my foot and mourning over the loss, I thought about my career as a social entrepreneur and professional speaker. I stopped asking "Why me?" and started asking "What for?"

With the added time I had available since I could not

run or even walk, I found a bigger problem or purpose than dwelling on my brokenness and expanded my creative talents, something that I never previously had time for. To be honest, I couldn't stand suffering any longer and needed to find a way to feel better. I finished a book I'd been working on for the past four years and developed new ideas as well, some of which would never have come to fruition if I had not broken my foot. This is tough to admit, but I realized that if running was my life, as I have said to myself and others countless times, then perhaps I should *get a life*. There is so much more to life than running; I was just not aware of it. Defining myself as a runner, or in any particular manner, is an excellent way to generate a LOT of pain. When we define ourselves by something, we're essentially telling ourselves that we're incomplete without it. However, this is totally false. We are entirely whole and complete in every way, regardless of how far we can run, or if we can run at all.

2. Get up! Do something. Take action and stop feeling sorry for yourself.

This may sound blunt, but it is reality. Stay in that place of mourning as long as you need to but not a moment longer. Eventually, we've got to get up!

Years ago, I was talking to my mom and crying the blues about something and she said, "If you are the only one attending your little pity party, you should leave." At the six month point after surgery, I took her advice and got up off the couch. I dug my sneakers out of the closet, went outside, and began to slowly put one foot in front of the other. In the past, if it was less than a ten kilometre run, I would not even bother lacing up my sneakers. Now I could not run at all, and my foot constantly throbbed in pain. However, the simple act of getting out in nature, limping along, and trying to run a tiny bit was a giant leap forward in my healing.

Everything changed in that moment. I had been saying to myself that I wanted to feel better, but I just stayed on the couch and wallowed in my own misery. Expecting things to get better when I stayed the same didn't work. Nothing changed until I got up off the couch, stopped feeling sorry for myself, and took action.

In businesses, it's the same thing. We must find a bigger problem than our own bottom line. Find a bigger purpose for your company than simply making money. Find a cause to support, something that everyone at work, even if it's only you and your customers, can get passionate about. Whether your passions are directly related to your business or not doesn't matter; when we find a bigger problem than our own bottom line, the excitement and inspiration we experience on a daily basis is contagious. Soon, others will jump on board and, remarkably, your business will profit. If you don't believe me, try it! Success is on the other side of service. Focusing on making a difference rather than simply making money is the key.

I know firsthand the influence of finding a bigger problem than my own bottom line. In all of my businesses, I've always divided my earnings in three categories: saving, spending, and sharing. I first heard this more than twenty years ago when I started my first business: an international travellers hostel. I had an audio cassette of Jim Rohn, a motivational speaker, and he said we must always reserve a portion of our earnings for charitable giving. And that's what I did. In my first year of business, I was so financially stretched as monthly mortgage payments on that property were in excess of $3000 per month, interest only. Christmas was coming and I had no money to buy big gifts for my staff. So, together we created a bigger problem – a bigger purpose – than ourselves. We scraped together about $100, called a local charity, and sponsored a family in need. With the money, my staff and I went out and bought toys and gifts for the family and wrapped them in newspaper and string. Then we took the items to the family, pretending to be delivery people. The joy and gratefulness they showed was the greatest Christmas gift I had ever received.

That was twenty years ago and every year, by helping others, I believe the Universe responds in kind. The mortgage on the hostel has long been repaid and I'm extremely grateful for the wealth I've received from the business and for the difference we've made in the world through the idea of saving, spending, and sharing. Charitable giving is a part of every speech, retreat, or workshop I offer. I will continue to focus on charitable giving as a bigger purpose for my businesses and life, not for what I get out of it, but for who I become in the process.

Make the Journey

At times in my life I have experienced agonizing self-doubt, insecurity, and overwhelming feelings of not being *enough*. These feelings of insignificance have given rise to certain ways of being that have actually helped me and propelled me forward in my life and business. For example, since I was very young I've been extremely independent. For as long as I can remember, I've also held a view that I can do anything I put my mind to through hard work. And I've always felt that life should be fair. These three ways of being have impacted my life in extraordinary ways! I've accomplished a lot, both personally and professionally, through the strength of these brilliant aspects of myself. However, left on autopilot in my subconscious, these three little devils can and do wreak havoc in my life in countless ways.

When an incident arises, like breaking my foot, it triggers all of my ways of being – of coping. Breaking my foot took away my independence for months. It showed me that I just might not be able to do anything I wanted through work ethic, grit, and determination, and it certainly ruined my ideal that life should be fair. It's easy to see why I was such a mess emotionally. I just could not make sense of it all through the filters that I had created to maneuver in life, and this only served to magnify my insecurity and self-doubt. The accident forced me to my knees and made me look at myself. Through that experience, I realized that there could be a better way.

There is a better way. It's a journey of knowing ourselves deeply, noticing when we are triggered, and choosing to breathe more space between that stimulus and our response. The better way is choosing to be vulnerable, to unabashedly allow our true selves to be seen, to create a gentle opening of the heart and mind, and to commit to the lifelong process of discovering and creating our best selves. It's a process of choosing compassion, authenticity, and love! This is so much easier said than done, but the journey of remembering who we are and knowing ourselves deeply will give rise to incredible abundance on every level.

Take a moment to be still and quiet. Think of your own ways of being. Who do you show up as in life? How do you interact with the world around you? Are you often defensive? Take things too personally? Overreact? What parts of you do you want the world to see, and what parts of you do you hide from those around you? What triggers you? Who do you become when you get triggered? See if you can clearly articulate and define your ways of being and gain clarity on how amazing those aspects of you are, while also being sabotaging little monsters at the same time. Simply becoming aware of the times when we are on autopilot will provide the space between stimulus and how we may choose to respond in a given situation.

As we strive to become our brilliant and best selves, we begin living our lives with intention rather than by default. As a result, our businesses will thrive, our staff will be happier, and our clients will be more motivated to work with us. Working harder on ourselves than on anything else will pay dividends in the long run.

Know Your Gifts, Talents, and Ultimate Purpose

It is our purpose in life to discover our unique gifts and talents and share them with the world. That is why we are here. Mark Twain said, "The two most important days in your life are the day you are born and the day you find out why." The day you find out why, your life will change – and so will the world!

Think about your gifts – not just what you are good at, but what energizes you to wake up early and go to bed late! Think of your passions, hobbies, business, and what inspires you. Think of what you are doing when time flies by so quickly that you lose track of it. Somewhere hidden there are your gifts – your innate gifts – and your reason for being here. Share them. The world needs you and what you have to offer, now more than ever.

It is essential that you know exactly what your gifts and talents are. If you are unclear on what your specific gifts and talents are, please contact me. I will send you an exercise via email that will bring clarity and focus for you on exactly why you are here, what your purpose is, and what you excel at.

When life goes completely and utterly sideways, and it

invariably will now and then, it's okay to *briefly* surrender to what the current state of things may be and to wallow in that. Surrendering is not about giving in or giving up, though. It is about acknowledging what is and moving beyond the suffering of wishing things could be different, of feeling like a victim, to a place of empowerment. To me, surrendering means to *become sure of the end* – to get a clear picture of the outcome you most desire, and then to surrender to that outcome and take action. As we surrender to whatever is happening in our lives, we begin to move from "why me" to "what for" in the direction of our most desired outcome.

We get closer to the "what for" side of things as we create new meaning, new discoveries, and new depths within our character as a result of going through and growing through whatever has taken place. As we create a bigger problem and as we make the journey from our heads to our hearts, sharing our innate gifts and talents, we will not only make more money, we will find everything we're seeking in life.

There are a few action steps that I've embarked upon that have made a world of difference in my life, and I am certain they will do the same for you.

1. **Take the 90-Day Challenge.** Pick two goals, large or small. Define them clearly. Set a start date and commit for ninety days. Every day, spend fifteen minutes completing three small steps towards those goals. Keep a journal to track your progress. The three action steps taken daily need only require a maximum of five minutes each to complete. Everyone has fifteen minutes they can find in a day, especially if you pick two goals that you are passionate about and not merely interested in.

2. **Make your health a priority.** Create a health goal as one of your goals in the 90-Day Challenge. Do something every day towards improving your health; you know what areas of your life need some attention. Spend a few minutes each day focusing on your health. You'll feel better, have more energy, and accomplish so much more as a result.

3. **Create a morning routine.** Again, this requires only fifteen minutes to one hour each morning to complete. Spend this time intentionally upon rising each day – meditate, grab a strong cup of coffee and set your intentions for the day, spend quality time with your partner and/or children in meaningful conversation, read, write, journal, exercise, write in a gratitude journal, connect with your spirituality, write a thank you card every morning for a year, and more. Commit to this routine for a month and watch your life change.

Moving from dwelling on my problems to finding a place of purpose took a long time for me. I suffered in the place of "Why me?" for months before being able to even consider the notion of "What for?" Do I wish the accident never happened? Absolutely! But would I want to give up all the incredible results that the accident generated: the personal growth, the wisdom gained, and who I've become through the past year? I don't think so. While the accident wreaked havoc in my life, it was also the catalyst for completing several projects. My work as a social entrepreneur, consultant, and speaker has been elevated as a result of the accident in many ways, not to mention the greater depth of my compassion and character. Organizations and companies hire me to work with their teams to become more productive, more inspired, and happier on a daily basis.

As a result of the accident, I know I can serve them better than I ever had before.

My wish for everyone is that when things happen in our lives that take us completely off the road we had planned, we may find the courage, the grace, and the vulnerability to surrender to what is, to intentionally choose how we respond in any given situation, to love ourselves in all our perfect imperfections, and to move from "Why me?" to "What for?" With this, we can use our gifts and talents to influence and change the world simply by showing up authentically, taking action, and bravely putting one foot in front of the other!

About Crystal Flaman

Social entrepreneur and athlete Crystal Flaman's personal mission in life is to make a difference in the world. She has raised over $1.4 million for various charities, including the Heart and Stroke Foundation of Canada, the Canadian Diabetes Association, and Room To Read through her work and athletic endeavors. She is an eleven-time Ironman finisher, a two-time 273 km ultra-marathoner finisher and has cycled across Canada with her twin sister on the first tandem bike to cross the country. She has also twice completed the second hardest footrace in the world - a 273 km multi-day, self-supported running race that goes through the Utah desert and over mountains.

Crystal is the owner of DIVA Retreats, the Kelowna International Hostel, and Inspiring Success Services Inc. She speaks around the world, inspiring audiences to reach their potential and achieve greater success and fulfillment in business and in life. She's the creator of "Imagine The Ripple Effect," The 90 Day Intentional Living Challenge and has recently written "Living The Dream (Simple Ideas To Live A Long, Healthy and Happy Life)." She's currently writing "A Secret Dream" in honour of the secret dreams in each of us.

Crystal's ultimate purpose in life is to inspire others to discover their own unique gifts and talents and share them with the world. She believes that as we move from success towards significance and from making money to what matters, share our innate talents, and listen to our intuition, we may find true joy, happiness, and fulfillment. She also believes that health is of utmost importance and that it's time to put our health first so that we may be able to live the long, healthy, and happy life we dream of and hope for.

www.inspiringsuccess.ca
Email: crystal@inspiringsuccess.ca
Telephone: 250-215-2903

3

FROM FINANCE TO FITNESS

by Mary Sayers

"Successful people have always found a mentor on their path towards success. Be open to someone supporting and encouraging you. The in-person mentors and your inner mentor called your intuition."
Marie Diamond

From Finance to Fitness

by Mary Sayers

My life experiences have taught me that your health is your true wealth! Taking control of your health, wellbeing, and fitness will empower you in many ways, from improving your self-esteem, confidence, and relationships with others to enabling you to work and play. The cost of being sick is very high – both financially and emotionally. For me, investing in being fit and healthy started in my teens and opened the door to a very rewarding career running my own fitness business, along with a few other surprises.

I was born in North Vancouver, where my British parents had moved to in 1956. Three daughters later, the family moved to Jersey, Channel Islands, which is located between England and France. The island is five by nine miles and famous for its Jersey cows, new potatoes, finance industry, and tourism.

Jersey was a fabulous place to be raised, and it is where my three brothers were born and we all went to school.

Spare tire

In the Spring of 1974, my parents decided to take their three teenage Canadian daughters on a trip back to Vancouver to revisit the land of their birth. We started in North Vancouver, where Mum and Dad were married and had their first house. Our adventure then continued with a road trip to Mons Lake in the Chilcotin wilderness, about eight hours north of Vancouver, where we stayed in a very rustic log cabin. Coming from Jersey, the majestic scenery of the forests, rivers, lakes, and mountains was simply stunning, and we were very impressed.

Then, there was the food. Breakfasts fit for a lumberjack, with stacks of pancakes – dripping with butter and maple syrup – accompanied by bacon and sausage. Chocolate chip cookies to snack on. The early evening brought something called "Happy Hour," which signaled that it was time for cocktails and accompanying plates of "chips and dip." I found myself eagerly participating in these eating and drinking bonanzas on a daily basis.

On the plane ride home, I remember tightening up the seat belt and, to my horror, discovering that I had accumulated a roll of blubber around my midsection that definitely wasn't there when I arrived. I also noticed that my jeans had mysteriously shrunk!

Horrified by my expanded girth, I sought out a diet book and embarked on my first structured attempt at weight loss. I followed the strict regime closely and in two weeks had lost the holiday surplus. However, I felt ghastly and tired, and I constantly craved all the foods that were not allowed on the regime. As soon as I was "off the diet," I resorted to binge eating as my body reacted to the starvation mode it had been placed in. Back came the weight and I ended up heavier than when I started!

This pattern continued for over a year, and all I learned from this experience is that **DIETING MAKES YOU FAT!** Not to mention sick, grumpy, tired, depressed, obsessed with food, and antisocial. For the first time in my life, I felt like a failure. I was out of control and heading for a serious eating disorder. I needed help. Fast. I couldn't spend my life obsessed with food, diets, and my weight. My health and sanity were at risk.

In desperation, I went to see my doctor, taking a little note with me that I had written earlier as I was afraid I wouldn't be able to get the words out. I asked for some "slimming pills," thinking that would be the solution. He looked at me and shook his head. "There are no such things," he said, and then took out a prescription pad and started writing.

He then handed me the "prescription" that was about to change my life. Scanning the words, I experienced a flood of mixed emotions when I realized that he had simply written "Join Weight Watchers."

I sat still and absorbed the information. Initially, I felt alarmed, realizing that I would have to declare my problem to a group of strangers, admit to being a dieting disaster, and commit to another weight loss plan! Then, a wave of relief came over me as I understood that this was exactly what I needed. My problem could never be solved by pills; what I required was mentoring, education, support, and a healthy lifestyle.

There was a Weight Watchers meeting running on Mondays. All of my diets had begun on Mondays so this would be a good day to start, although this would be a much different approach!

That was in January 1977. I was eighteen and weighed

around 142 pounds. Being 5'4" with a petite frame, I was told my goal weight would be 112 pounds. All the staff at the meeting had been through the program, were successful, and had a passion to share their experience with others. I was inspired, relieved, excited, and optimistic. I soon came to realize that it wasn't me who was the failure, it was the diets! Restricting my food and then returning to my previous unhealthy eating patterns was not the answer.

The first week on the program I dropped four pounds and was amazed as I had eaten so much food! Sadly, about 95% of people who lose weight will regain it in under a year, but I was determined that I would be one of the 5%.

Over the next five months I attended my weekly meetings, weighed and measured my portions, kept my weekly food planner, and always stayed to listen to the talks on how to navigate this journey successfully. I had found the mentorship I needed and a support group of like-minded people. This was a life-changing experience in so many ways. I was empowered.

Of course, there were good days and bad days, as well as weeks where my weight increased or stayed the same, but I understood this was part of the process and stuck with it. The Weight Watchers program ultimately changed my life as I discovered that I could do anything that I set my mind to.

The definition of self-esteem is that it reflects a person's overall subjective emotional evaluation of his or her own **worth**. It is a judgment of oneself as well as an attitude towards the self. It encompasses beliefs about oneself, such as "I am competent" or "I am **worthy**." My health and happiness were important to my self-esteem, and they were well worth investing in.

My struggle to be slim had transitioned into an ongoing process of becoming healthier and happier. I reached my goal weight in five months, discarding thirty pounds, and have maintained it (give or take five pounds) ever since.

Finding Fitness

Weight Watchers encouraged us to increase our exercise and activity levels to complement the food plan, so I sought out some fitness classes. "Popmobility" and "Bar Belles" were the two classes I enrolled in, the former being a dance to music class and the latter a circuit training class in a gym using barbells and dumbbells. I probably wouldn't have signed up if it had been called "Dumb Belles"!

I immediately loved these classes. I had found something to be passionate about again; something that was fun, made me feel good, and helped me lose fat and increase my lean muscle mass. The exercise also helped me look and function better and become stronger, fitter, more toned, and more flexible. I was hooked! After a year, my Popmobility instructor retired and handed the class over to me as I had shown an aptitude to teach movement. Looking back, this was the start of my fitness career.

Soon I was experiencing a new confidence that stirred up something deep inside. My gut was telling me I had to take a leap of faith and expand my horizons. There was something I needed to do, and it wasn't in Jersey.

1984 was a pivotal point in my life. At the age of twenty-five I had a secure and well-paying job, had been in a solid relationship for eight years, and was able to afford two incredible holidays every year. But I wasn't feeling fulfilled, and I knew this wasn't the career I craved or the man I would marry. Looking to my father for advice, he suggested that I take out a piece of paper, divide it into two columns and list the reasons as to why I would either stay or go. It was strangely easy.

I had a yearning to make a big move and leave Jersey. I craved a career in a profession that would be both challenging and rewarding, but I still had no clue what it would be! Being a Canadian citizen by birth, I applied for my passport and booked a flight to Vancouver. And so began an exciting new chapter in my life.

After a succession of office jobs in several financial institutions, I was getting concerned that I still didn't have a career path. I remember commenting to a co-worker that I needed a change. She looked up from the newspaper she had been glancing through and replied that she had just seen a job advertised for a fitness consultant position at a women-only gym in North Vancouver. Time for a big change! I applied for and got the job. Suddenly a new path opened for me, and within a year I was promoted to the position of manager.

I also started working for Weight Watchers as a leader. Having had sedentary office jobs for a few years, I had regained some weight and needed a refresher on the program that had previously helped me. As a lifetime member, I returned to the meetings, got back to my goal weight, and was then asked if I would be interested in working for the organization. With no hesitation, I completed the training program and started leading meetings part-time in North Vancouver. I held this position for over ten years whilst I also worked as a personal trainer and group fitness instructor. I was helping others, and this was very meaningful to me. I had found a career in the fitness industry and I loved my work.

Becoming a MOD

1988 was the 25th anniversary of the Weight Watchers organization, and to honour this milestone they launched a contest called Members of the Decade (or MODs) to find the top success stories in each decade since its inception. Two representatives were to be chosen for the 60's, 70's and 80's, and they would be featured at the big celebrations taking place in New York that September. They weren't looking for the biggest change in weight, but rather for inspirational stories that represented the benefits and changes that can come from being on the program, with an emphasis on long-term success at keeping the weight off.

I applied and was selected as one of the winners for the 70's! Articles about us were featured on TV and in newspapers and magazines, and I was awarded an all-expenses paid trip for two to New York. This included accommodations at the Waldorf Astoria plus a spending allowance to go shopping, and I was fortunate to share this truly incredibly experience with my younger sister. It was definitely a high point in my life, and an achievement I was very proud of.

Mind your Own Business

My belief is that we are put on this planet to support and serve others and to be happy. I always knew I would be an entrepreneur; it was just something I sensed, deep inside.

In my thirties I had developed a successful career in the fitness industry, which I knew was the place I wanted to be, but I wasn't very happy working for other people and organizations. My creativity was suppressed and I was constantly commuting between different facilities.

Now approaching my forties, I was looking for another change and discovered Pilates. With great enthusiasm, I completed an instructor training certification program in San Francisco. Being a mind-body discipline with a strong emphasis on posture, alignment, breathing, and core strength, I knew this was a method that would help many people get out of pain and become more active. It changed how I looked, felt, and moved, and I was eager to share its benefits with others.

My instincts told me that this was the work I needed to focus on, and I recognized that I would become an entrepreneur and open my own studio. Naturally I had lots of doubts, so once again I got out a piece of paper, divided it in two, and made my lists of pros and cons. Once again, it was strangely easy. I was going to be a business owner, just like my Dad. I would work long hours, be my own boss, and be successful!

In September, 1999, I opened the Esprit de Core Fitness Studio in West Vancouver. The months leading up to its launch were a roller coaster of learning experiences, and I was very fortunate to have had some amazing people around to support me. Thankfully, the business took off in a way I had never anticipated. We were extraordinarily busy, and I had a lot of learning to do. I was not only teaching most of the classes but also running the business, cleaning the facility, and attempting to balance the books!

I had to work long hours, but it was worth it. My time and effort paid off as we became an established business with hundreds of clients experiencing very positive changes. Health professionals were referring clients to us as we were having great success with back care and core conditioning programs. Pilates was hugely popular and we had found a niche market.

However, after a few years, the "busyness of the business" started to catch up with me and I was struggling with burnout.

My adrenals were exhausted and my life was out of balance. The business was profitable and I was giving it my all, but at what cost?

"C" – Not Me!

In 2003, I changed to a new dentist. At my first check-up I was informed that there was a tiny mark on the underside of my tongue that looked unusual, and I was advised to have a biopsy and get it checked out. Always being a big believer in preventative measures where health is concerned, I went for it. When the results came back I was told I had "Squamous Cell Carcinoma," a very rare cancer under my tongue. Yes, CANCER. I was stunned!

This was devastating news. I felt numb, shocked, and horrified. I immediately had visions of losing my curly blonde locks, which are a big part of my identity. I would be bald. Perhaps I would die.

"The Lucky One" was the nickname the lovely ladies at the cancer agency gave me. I was told that I was very lucky to have an attentive dentist, to have had an early diagnosis, to not need chemo and radiation, and to have such great hair, which I wouldn't lose! So lucky me had oral surgery and the tumour was removed. My tongue healed quickly, and I came away with a new lease on life.

In the following months, I made mental and physical health my priority. I ended a relationship with a great man who just wasn't the guy for me, cut back my hours, delegated more work, travelled more, and had more fun. Working with a naturopath, I made positive changes to what I ate, fine-tuned my supplements, and focused on reducing my stress levels and improving my immunity. One goal was to sail through menopause, and I crushed it! My fifties were going to be awesome. No mid-life crisis for me!

I truly believe that mismanaged stress triggered the cancer. Being on my tongue suggested a blockage of healing energy in my throat, which is the communication center. For several years I had a succession of uniquely challenging people in my life who I struggled to communicate with. If only I had recognized this, I might have got help sooner. What I have learnt is to ask for help.

Regularly participating in personal growth programs has always been a passion of mine. Being in the fitness business inspired me to attend ongoing training workshops and to continue to embrace new programs, for the benefit of both myself and my clients.

Over ten years ago I found out about WOW and attended the conference in Vancouver. It was such a fun, inspiring and empowering event, and I was hooked. Having attended every subsequent conference, I claim to be the most WOWed woman in Vancouver!

A Bride at Fifty-One

In the summer of 2008, I was at an outdoor Latin music concert in West Vancouver when a charming man made his way over to me and asked me to dance. The rest is history, as they say. James and I were married in Jersey in 2010. I was fifty-one and it was the best day of my life!

Looking back, my life has been an amazing adventure of ups and downs, challenges and successes. I turn sixty this year, and will have been running my own business for over twenty years! I am proud of all of my accomplishments and failures. They have led me to becoming an inspired entrepreneur, wife, daughter, step-mother, and optimist. Discovering the value of my health at a young age was one of my greatest blessings. Strangely, getting the cancer diagnosis was too.

Helping others to feel fitter and function better is my purpose and passion. My work is very rewarding and gives me a lot of satisfaction. It feels amazing to know that you have a positive influence on others. By being an entrepreneur, I have found abundance and feel fulfilled, proud, and happy.

There are many lessons I've learned in my life. Listen to the voice inside and trust your instincts. Make lists and plans, and then take action. Attitude is everything, so smile and have FUN! Never stop learning, growing, and becoming a better you. Seek out other people, such as experts and mentors, to guide you on your journeys. And of course, don't forget to invest in being fit and healthy. Take control of your health, and you will see benefits in all aspects of your life. That is your true wealth.

About Mary Sayers

Mary has always enjoyed an active lifestyle and feels very fortunate to have lived in places where there are abundant opportunities for indoor and outdoor recreation. Health, fitness, and the joy of movement have always been her passion, and she started teaching group fitness classes at the age of eighteen.

The most difficult times in her life revolved around health issues. By facing and overcoming these challenges, Mary has gained a wealth of knowledge about how to obtain optimal wellness and be fit, healthy, and happy. She has learned that her purpose and passion in life is to inspire and educate others who are wanting to make positive changes in their health and fitness.

In 1999, Mary decided to become an entrepreneur and opened the Esprit de Core Fitness Studio in Ambleside, West Vancouver. With over forty years of teaching fitness, Mary has selected Pilates, CoreAlign, and the MELT Method to be the programs she specializes in. The results are impressive and Mary practices what she preaches.

With her guidance and support, Mary's clients benefit from better posture, restored movement, reduced pain and stiffness, and improved overall fitness, flexibility, and balance. She believes that even small improvements can be beneficial and that it is never too late to start!

Mary is blessed to live and work in West Vancouver. She is a keen gardener who loves good food, dancing, and travel. She believes in a positive attitude, learning, and having fun, and that KNOWLEDGE combined with ACTION are the keys to success!

www.espritdecore.com
Email: info@espritdecore.com
Facebook: Mary Sayers or Esprit de Core Fitness Studio Ltd
Instagram: esprit_de_core
LinkedIn: linkedin.com/in/mary-sayers-06a8a918

4

THE TIP OF THE ICEBERG

by Gilly Thomas

"Doesn't everything die at last, and too soon?
Tell me, what do you plan to do
With (the rest of) your one wild and precious life?"
Mary Oliver

The Tip of the Iceberg

by Gilly Thomas

Self-awareness is one of those elusive concepts. I love the metaphor of an iceberg; we only see what's above the surface, but there is far more hiding in the waters below. How can I be aware of what I can't see? How can anyone? There are bookshelves and Google searches full of work from psychologists who have spent lifetimes studying why people are blind to the obvious. Jung called it "Shadow Work," while Freud called it "resistance." I like the iceberg because I'm Canadian, and because when energy gets stuck it can feel like ice.

This feeling can be a relief; a numbness that makes the pain recede, and even though life is bland, blank, and grey, at least there is no more anguish. This is where I found myself when I started my journey into unwrapping my pain. What I didn't realize at the time what that the agony I was feeling was wrapped in an overwhelming sense of sadness, which I was absorbing from the world around me.

It takes courage to turn around, melt the ice, and feel the pain without knowing that the other side exists; the side that is full of sunshine, hope, laughter, and love. To do this, I needed to get in touch with my fear, love, anger, sadness, and shame. Not to just experience them, but to rejoice in them; that's where emotional intelligence lives.

What is intelligence anyway? Well, there are several different types. Cognitive intelligence is defined as "the ability to acquire and apply knowledge and skills." In contrast, emotional intelligence is being able to know your emotions, along with the emotions of others, and then use this insight to guide thought and action. Energetic intelligence is being able to identify the energy of yourself and others and use this acuity to read emotions and take action to move from held energy (potential) to energy in motion (kinetic).

I was chatting with an old friend over a cup of tea today and mentioned that I was working on my chapter for this book. She asked what it was about, and I told her I was writing about my journey of discovering that I am an empath and how it affects my personal and work life. At that point she asked, "What do you mean, empath?"

I smiled and explained that I feel other people's energy, emotion, and physical sensations very clearly in myself. For example, if there is a funeral and I'm walking down the street a couple of blocks away, I feel a big wave of sadness that washes right over me. I'm not actually sad; I could even be happy! However, at that moment there's sad energy, and I pick it up. And it's not just emotional energy. Another time, I was sitting in an airport and reading a book. I was engrossed in the story and feeling comfy in my body when a family sat down behind me. Instantly, I felt an excruciating pain in my back. I shifted to try and move it, but the pain stayed with me until I got up and physically moved a distance away. I found this interesting, so I decided to experiment and move back to where I'd been sitting. Boom, the pain was back in full force.

I used to be tuned into this energy all the time; it was overwhelming, and I didn't understand what was going on. At one point I was instructed to build a barrier to block the energy that caused my discomfort as a way of protecting myself, but that took a lot of resistance and effort. Now I don't judge or stop it, because it's just energy unless there's a value attached to it. I've learned to check in with myself and take care of myself; then I can be clear in listening to what is happening for my clients.

I love my work, because that's when I bring my awareness into myself and turn up the volume of my response. This allows me to feel whether energy is flowing within my client or stuck. When energy flows there is a sense of bounce and ease, while stuck energy is generally feels dense, cold, or very hot. It can manifest as physical or emotional patterns that are painful. I now tune into these states of being when I do the hands-on work as a bodymind therapist, which serves to guide me as I work with people. I have learned how to use myself as a gauge.

As an empath, I have had to find ways that my business worked with my life and vice versa. There are a few things I've discovered along the way that give me strength, courage, and perseverance. The educations I've received were both formal and informal, and my life lessons are the foundation for who I am and how I do business. Even though it wasn't easy to get to where I am now, I followed my gut and found ways to make things happen.

A Journey Under the Water

All of my life, I had felt deeply sad. As I've come to understand, the energy of sadness wrapped up all of my other emotions. Most people know only one or two of their emotions; the rest are hidden under the surface. Some people hide under anger, while others put on a façade of happiness. For me, I bundled all of my emotions – and the emotions of others – in sadness.

I had yet to understand that I absorbed the energy of others the way a sponge soaks up water, so I was constantly seeking a way to understand the world. When I was in my late twenties, I was told about the Rubenfeld Synergy Method. RSM is about the interrelation of body, mind, emotions, and spirit, and used a combination of touch and talk to bring awareness to all of those dimensions. The problem was that the training was in New York, it took four years, and it was expensive. I decided I'd wait until my daughter went to school, which would give my husband and I the time to save and prepare for me being away for extended periods of time.

I spoke with my Mum about the program and my plan. She looked at me first with delight and then shock before saying, "You've been looking for this your whole life. Why would you wait another moment to start?" That's my Mum. She embodies the phrase, "you can think about it until the cows come home, but if you don't do anything, nothing will actually change."

She also has this great philosophy that obstacles will be overcome in ways that you cannot foresee. Finances, childcare, and other practical things would work themselves out somehow. Believing this, I applied right away, and when I was accepted I went for it.

Through the process of study and beyond, I continued

to struggle with my sadness. I began to gain some deeper awareness, including:

1. All of my emotions were bundled in sadness.
2. My sadness was intergenerational and womb-deep.
3. Emotional pain and physical pain are related.
4. Energy moves through physical barriers and when it gets stuck, it stops.
5. Energetic intelligence is my gift.

As these became clear, I began to feel the emotions and energy of love, joy, fear, anger, and excitement. My physical body was no longer tight and tense from trying to hold things in. As I discovered the value of all emotions and began to enjoy the resulting feeling of energetic flow, I became comfortable in my own skin.

Ripples

After graduating, I built a solid practice as a bodymind therapist and public speaker in Alberta. Nowadays mind-body connection and psycho-somatic processing are better understood, but back in the day it was an unfamiliar concept. If you felt physical pain, you saw a doctor; for mental distress, a psychologist or psychiatrist. Energy was still unknown and considered woo-woo. I love teaching, so I began educating people on the benefits of this holistic approach at every opportunity. My private practice was full, with people travelling from around the province and across the country to see me. I was even sought out as a public speaker!

Then came an unexpected twist. I was deeply in love with my husband and was accustomed to the rollercoaster that was my marriage, so I didn't really think that life would or could be different. Our relationship lasted eleven years before the ride finally ended in 2004. We had a beautiful daughter, a home, friends, mutual work interests, and a life together. Coming apart from the marriage was incredibly painful, left me feeling raw and vulnerable, and turned my life upside-down.

My ten-year-old daughter was affected by our separation, and she became angry and non-communicative. While my work was important to me, my relationship with my daughter as she neared her teen years was vital. I knew this intimately as I'd been a junior/senior high school teacher for several years prior to becoming a bodymind therapist. Typically, the early teen years are a time of great upheaval for children as they leave the cocoon of elementary school and, full of hormones, enter the world of high school. It is a new beginning and a time for growth and expansion. I wanted my daughter to foster her independence with confidence, and not become stuck in anger.

However, my work gave me stability, security, consistency, and an income. Contrary to popular belief, Albertans embraced alternative therapy and being at the leading edge gave me an open field. I could have stayed safe and continued living where I was, building my business but feeling a lack of connection in my personal life. Unfortunately, the divorce had disconnected me from my inner gauge. I had known how I felt in my marriage, and I knew how my inner self felt – emotionally, physically, and energetically – when I was in that primary relationship. When it ended, I wasn't sure where my gauge pointed anymore. In order to tune into the inner states of my clients, I need to be clear about what my internal clues are. When I feel stuck, then I cannot guide my clients to greater awareness and choice and I am doing a disservice to both my clients and myself. What to do?

First and foremost, I decided that I needed to take care of my family. I explained to my daughter that she was super lucky as she now had two families: one with me, and one with her Dad. I asked her what she'd love to do. One answer was to ride on horseback and the other was to travel. Funny, those were two of my passions as well. It became apparent very quickly that riding was not the best choice, as she was terribly allergic to horses! So instead, we turned to travel.

Feel the Fear and Melt It

The kind of travel I wanted to do was not your typical two-week vacation; I had only ever done extended adventures, including working across Canada and around the globe. I was lucky as my ex-husband was a mountain guide who journeyed far and wide with clients. He understood the value of learning in different countries, so he was on board with our daughter having that experience at a young age.

There is something to be said about being afraid and doing it anyway. The night before I left Canada, my lawyer brought the divorce papers over for me to sign and said that while I felt like I was divorced, legally I wasn't. She also said I'd feel differently once it was all said and done. I signed with a shrug and a "thanks." Months later I got the word that everything was finalized, and she was right; there was a weight off my shoulders when the divorce was "official." It can feel scary to really complete a circle, but once it's done, it's done and there is no more fear.

I headed off into the wide blue yonder with my daughter as my backup. Our general plan was that we would start in Australia because it was an English-speaking country and one that she wanted to visit. Here we would figure out our modus operandi for travelling, and then we'd head to our next stop. I chose Thailand for the climbing, the price point, and to write a book; the small village we stayed in was far enough away from everything "normal" that I could focus on my writing. It was also close to Myanmar, where my Mum was born, and I wanted to trace some family roots.

We had many adventures and no regrets. The time away brought my daughter and I back into a good relationship, and I also had the time and space to reconnect with myself. After experiencing deep grief, I was reminded of how vast the world is and how many opportunities there are to be alive. We did everything we wanted to do, from scuba diving on the Great Barrier Reef, to taking a train to northern Myanmar, to going to the Palace of Versailles. Anything either of us thought would be interesting, fun, or an adventure, we did. Why hold back?

This year of life lessons gave me the fortitude to move to Vancouver. I wanted my daughter to be comfortable living in and navigating a big city. I also wanted to meet someone and have a long-term relationship. Living in my small town… honestly, at my age all the good guys were married so my options were limited. Love was the scariest emotion to feel again because it had been the most painful. However, I had rediscovered that when you face your fear and do it anyway, wonderful things happen.

What I didn't realize was that all the work I'd put into building my business in Alberta had done a lot to get me established, and now I would have to start over. People were loyal to their alternative therapy practitioners, such as massage therapists or chiropractors, and did not feel the need to see someone new and different. I was back to square one and having to connect, educate, and extend myself to find work.

Take Action Through Emotion and Energy

Emotion is energy-in-motion. When our emotions get stuck, then the energy goes from being kinetic energy to potential energy. What is possible? Nothing, if action isn't taken. In fact, the opposite happens because it takes energy to stop energy! Imagine that you had a large reserve of energy and in order to keep it contained, you have to keep pushing it down. This can result in "dis-ease" such as depression, chronic fatigue, or cancer. The physical or mental manifestation of held trauma can be devastating or simply decrease your ability to love life.

For example, a client in her thirties was enraged at all men, all of the time. She knew that men triggered her but had no recollection of what might be at the root of her rage. She constantly held herself in, because her anger was out of proportion to her daily situations. As a result, she was exhausted or "depressed." After several bodymind therapy sessions, where we tapped into her cellular memory, it came to light that she was sexually abused for most of her childhood. When her rage was expressed at the perpetrator, she slowly returned to life in the present and there was room for other emotions to emerge. She began to enjoy interactions with men, both at work and socially. Her life changed.

Another client laid on the table and began a metaphorical journey into her heart. There was a dark, deep forest that had no path, and she wound her way through the trees until she arrived at a dilapidated old building. All of the windows and doors were closed, with wooden slats nailing them shut. Immediately every cell in her body tensed; she was terrified. After some reassurance and encouragement, she approached the building and pried one slat off a window. Her whole body sprang away on the table and she began to shake uncontrollably. I asked what was there. The answer came: "My smile." At the end of the session, she sat up and was beaming from ear to ear. She told me that when she was a young child she had buck teeth and her family told her not to smile and to hide her ugly teeth. She became quiet and never smiled…until now, in her mid fifties. There are a multitude of ripple effects from not smiling; the physical act of smiling releases serotonin (the feel-good hormone) in your brain, and without it, emotionally, you feel sad. That session taught me that I never know what someone could be afraid of, or what was frozen below the surface of their subconscious.

I also worked with a professional athlete who had severe upper back pain that kept him off the field for three months. He had seen many of the physical modality professionals, including a massage therapist, physiotherapist, chiropractor, and sports medicine doctor. During the session with me, he felt a sharp triangle digging into his upper back and related that to his coach, his mother, and himself. I asked what the triangle could be instead; he breathed, and his back softened. The triangle had metamorphosed into a circle. His physical issue had an emotional root, and once it transformed he could return to play. This is another example of an inter-relation between physical and emotional states.

I reach out and touch people in my work, both literally and figuratively, to shine a light of awareness on what is frozen under the surface. As the ice melts it creates healing ripples that reach many, because when you allow yourself to be alive then others can be too. My own journey has been long; getting stuck and unstuck can be a process! It is still ongoing, truth be told, but it no longer overwhelms or scares me. I now enjoy the adventure.

About Gilly Thomas, CRS, BEd, BA

Gilly is an intuitive bodymind healer, sensitive empath, grassroots philanthropist, outdoor enthusiast, tough broad, fierce competitor, team player, fast driver, adventurer, bicycle commuter, and passionate conversationalist who has an expertise and depth of being that you will benefit from. She is a firm, fair, and loving mother and stepmother and a fun-loving, active wife.

Gilly works with the interrelation of body, mind, emotions, energy and spirit. No part of you is left out of your wellness equation. She is a Certified Rubenfeld Synergist, with a background in education, psychology, and nursing, and has worked in the field of wellness for over twenty years.

Using her finely-tuned and highly sensitized body/brain/heart instrument, Gilly facilitates healing for others by helping them access and release unseen and unspoken traumas and challenges that keep them unfulfilled. She moves people towards living comfortably in their skin by shining the light under water so they can discover the rest of their iceberg, melt the fear, and live the range of beauty within.

In addition to her private practice and online courses, she presents workshops and lectures in Canada and the USA. Her method of delivering experiential and intellectual content ensures you will "get it from the inside out."

www.workingwithwellness.ca
www.urbuildingknowledge.com
Facebook: @WorkingWithWellnessVancouver
Instagram: working_with_wellness

5

WOMAN OF VALUE –
NO MATTER WHAT

by Mary Pichette

"Character cannot be developed in ease and quiet. Only through experience of trial and suffering can the soul be strengthened, vision cleared, ambition inspired and success achieved."
Helen Keller

Woman of Value – No Matter What

by Mary Pichette

Like all people, I have a story to tell. I survived childhood abuse. I coped for many years by using heroin and other drugs; I loved being high and dead to my feelings. I was bought and sold by awful and violent men, and I blamed myself for all of my wrongdoings. In the early 70's, the words to talk about my pain had not been used yet. Being female and an addict, there were no groups or places to go for detoxing or counselling. The onus was on me to keep the secrets and "stay silent," no matter what. The life I was required to portray was one that was filled with achievement and purity, so that's what I portrayed.

I eventually found a listener, a person who believed me, and thus began my journey to living drug-free and abuse-free. Yet twenty-five years later, I was incredibly lonely, divorced, and realizing that despite all the changes I had worked to make, I was without any real success in nurturing healthy, caring relationships. In fact, I seemed to be surrounded by drama, stories, endlessly distraught friendships, and love that was filled with betrayal. I did well in work, but there too I seemed to put myself into messes.

I continued to stress about, and be frustrated with, my friendships. I never felt like I was understood; I always felt like the "outsider." I still was not believed by my family when I spoke about the ongoing abuses and violence in my life, and I seemed to only get so far in my relationships before the patterns would repeat. After getting divorced, I once again found myself in an abusive relationship. I just couldn't "get it."

In order to move forward, I started asking questions. Questions about how to relate with people. How to be angry without "seeing red." How to feel innocence and have fun. How to state what I needed so I could get what I wanted instead of trying to please everyone.

I have made all the relationship mistakes one can make, and I wanted better. I wanted healthy relationships in all aspects of my life. I wanted this cycle to stop. I was tired of the hurt, betrayal, and abuses, so I set out to find what a "healthy" relationship was like. I did everything humanly possible to create positive, beneficial relationships for myself.

What I discovered was that I was never without feelings; I had simply buried them in the darkest hole I could possibly create. If anything, I was too sensitive, alert, and hyper-vigilant when I was young. I experienced too much betrayal. As a child, I was raped at a summer camp by the "godly" catholic priest. I told the morning nun and was promptly strapped; at that point, I made a decision to NEVER speak of what happened again. I would not cry or allow the hurt and betrayal caused by the priest – and by my disbelieving parents – to be felt again.

I fought back against my feelings of sadness, loneliness,

and fear. I became very head-strong. I fed my intellect by reading books and I talked a lot, maybe too much! I was never still, trying anything to stay away from feeling. Eventually the "anything" became drugs. I also accepted and believed that I must go along with any and all sex forced on me; eventually, men started giving money to my "boyfriend" so I could engage in on-demand sexual favors.

Then one day I was asked, "Mary, don't you feel that?" I said no.

"That" was a two-inch gash in my leg, which was bleeding profusely with a few splinters of wood sticking out. No, I didn't feel the pain of the injury until someone else – someone outside of my body – said "that" must hurt. Then, and only then, did I experience a horrible feeling of pain. I had a whole lot of physical pains that I rarely felt, and I certainly never felt the emotional ones. This made me come across as "strong" and "determined," when in fact I was just numb.

At the time of the injury, I was in a training course focused on "Identifying Feelings." When my brain and the pain in my leg finally connected, I realized that the physical pain was a "feeling," and feelings were clearly something I needed to work on.

This kickstarted my adventure in discovering how to express my feelings. At first I was able to say I felt bad, sore, dead inside, numb, empty, and tired. For a while, that's as far as I could get. At varying moments within the following days and weeks I began stating feelings I could label that were physical. I feel tight. I feel nauseous. I feel pain in my leg.

When I was consciously able to acknowledge that I had a "feeling," I would then work with myself until I found the right label for it. As I expanded my feeling vocabulary, I acknowledged "I feel alone," "I feel excited," and "I feel nervous and jumpy."

Bit by bit, I labelled a new feeling here and acknowledged a new feeling there. I began to understand myself, and from this I could better understand others.

This represents only a small and incremental part of my skills training, something I had been missing after all my therapy and "treatment": the skills I needed to effectively relate to others and create healthy relationships. How could I understand you when I couldn't express my own feelings? Inch by inch, I began the second journey of my wonderful life: training to be a life skills coach, and eventually becoming a trainer of life skills coaches, so I could effectively teach what I had learned and help others practice and use the skills needed to enjoy life.

As I extended my training and coaching practice, I soon realized that I was not alone. So many women and men were in the same situation as me. They had spent many years healing from addictions, abuse, and family trauma that lead to PTSD, but had still not learned the skills they needed to relate and communicate with others.

Now, let me introduce you to that single most life-changing lesson I received as I was training and experiencing greater and greater depth in how to relate effectively. It was the moment I was told I was a whole and complete woman of value. Period.

I did not, and could not, "earn" my own worth and value. I did not have to undo the past, nor did I have to make up for it. I couldn't. Nonetheless, I had been on the treadmill of trying to "get better" and improve myself so I could be valued. I didn't need to "get better," though; as far as my value as a woman went, I *was* "better." You do not have to earn or become a woman of value, you have always been one. You don't need to "fix" your past to be deserving of your worth.

Bear in mind, as a girl who has been sexually abused and a

young woman who has been bought and sold, I felt like I had a lot to "make up" for. To any woman who has survived abuse, violence, sexual assault, addiction, destructive eating, and more: believe me when I say that anyone who has had these experiences in their life knows the mountains and mountains of shame and guilt attached. My life-changing moment was being told, "It is a FACT that you, Mary, are a whole and complete woman of value. NO MATTER WHAT!"

I started to realize other people could benefit from this message, so I began asking other women that I met in my community of recovery and social work, "Do you feel like a whole and complete woman of value, right now, right this minute?" Almost everyone one of them said no – professionals, students, and clients alike.

So, I began to explain that no matter if you've lived the beat-up life of abuse, exploitation, addiction and recovery, you are a whole and complete woman of value. If you've lived the holiest, most perfect, mistake-free life, you are also a whole and complete woman of value. It is not about how we "feel"; some days you bounce with positive self-esteem, and other days not so much. No matter what path we walk or how we feel about ourselves, we are all equal in value and worth.

In order to help others learn and accept this important message, I developed specialized curriculums for women overcoming PTSD. As we began our group sessions, we learned that most days these women feel depressed and disgusted with themselves. The experience of female trauma imprints messages of shame and self-loathing onto the frontal cortex. I would encourage them to start saying "I am a whole and complete woman of value" when they woke up, when they went to sleep, and all throughout the day. No matter what they felt, no matter what their behaviours are or were, their value and worthiness does not change. EVER.

Most of us, men and women alike, wait until we wake up one day "feeling" valuable, whole, and complete. When we constantly tell ourselves that we already have worth and value, day by day we will come to believe this truth. Eventually, we will feel it. We must very specifically work with our brains to replace the messages and frozen fear of trauma and re-program ourselves, as it were, with the truth of being whole and complete women and men of value. In my courses, this message replacement is effective because it is combined with ongoing, sequenced, and experiential lessons in life skills.

I was born a child of value and worth, as were you. All the nonsense of my "past" does not change that. I wanted a more emotionally balanced life, and I know this is what the women I was helping wanted too. However, the goal isn't to "arrive" and feel whole and complete at all times, in every circumstance. It is simply to know this as a fact, and to come to believe it.

With this knowledge and so many more lessons, I have become healthy and effective in my relationships. How do I know my relationships are working?

1. I enjoy spending time with myself and my friends, family, colleagues, neighbours, and community.
2. I have a strong faith and I know who I am in relation to God. My spiritual life is rich and strong in prayer, fellowship, and support.
3. I can, and do, ask others for help now and then. I seek out feedback and want to know what I might do to be more helpful in relating to other people in my life.
4. I feel cared for in ways that are special and unique to each of the people I choose to be in relationship with.

5. I am not in constant anxiety because I am afraid of conflict, misunderstandings, anger, failure, fault, or making a mess of things.
6. I trust myself to be in charge of how I act and feel in relationships with my friends, family, business associates, and community. Am I perfect? Not on your life! However, I trust that I can be transparent, and I am willing to work through what may have gone wrong and share in what we are doing right.
7. I celebrate and appreciate my daily life; most days, I am happy to be me!

Today, my passion is telling every woman she is a whole and complete woman of value. No matter what. No matter the losses, the mistakes, the misadventures, the lies, the faults of everything she's done or been; she is a whole and complete woman of value, no matter what. She also cannot ever earn her value with the perfect cupcakes, the perfect timing, the perfect grades, the great profits, or the brilliant ideas; it is a fact of life that exists for all of us. She does not need to believe it, or even feel it. She needs to simply know it, and to run forward from there. This message is not just important for women though; I work with many men, and I give them the exact same message. They have value and worth, no matter what.

When talking with people who are recovering from trauma, I am asked over and over, "Mary, what does a healthy relationship look like? All I learned was survival and coping. I hate all that addiction and PTSD has done to me, my family, my life, and continues to do to my relationships."

"Mary, what did you do to escape? To change?"

Having heard these questions or ones like them a thousand times, I left my career as a social worker and set about pouring myself into creating my Powerful Connection Mastery Program. This program captures all the learning and training of my life. I teach the skills of how to have healthy relationships in order to break the chains of generations who have poor skills – or no skills – and no knowledge of what a healthy relationship even looks like. For the past twenty-five years, I have reached out wherever and whenever I can to teach and show people how to relate effectively in ALL our relationships.

In my programs, I teach how to resolve conflict without resorting to rage or withdrawal, and how to understand the difference between a values-based conflict and a misunderstanding. People learn how to ask effective questions so they can actually get to know someone, and how to listen effectively to reduce misunderstandings and denial. By focusing on skill development, I help others gain the skills to effectively solve people problems across the various relationships in their lives.

However, an important and significant part of my journey is the development of my current speaking and training business, which allowed me to introduce and deliver my life skills training programs to the charity I was leading from 1998 to 2013. For fifteen years we ran very successful experiential programs, working with women who survived human trafficking to teach them the skills they needed to relate and connect effectively. We offered safe homes to women and girls and operated a full-time education centre which they attended every day. At this centre, they learned about defining a relationship, using words to effect conflict management, setting out life plans, how to solve problems effectively, and how to tell others what they needed to feel supported. The afternoons were spent in academic classes that gave government-authorized credits for Grade Ten, Eleven, and Twelve courses.

One of the guiding principles of our charity was that "when you educated a woman, you changed a generation." It is important, though, that this education extends past traditional school curriculums to include learning healthy relationship skills which can be transferred and put into practical use in everyday life. When you have the skills to relate effectively and can nourish healthier relationships, your brain can take in more educational information. It is not distracted by the drama and chaos of seeking approval and "love" in order to feel of worthy. The courageous women and girls staying in our safe homes knew they were whole and complete women of value, without needing a boyfriend or girlfriend to tell them so.

The women who graduated from our educational centre were able to maintain the changes they learned. They have gone on to successful careers and pursued post secondary education. Our charity was twice awarded The Donner Foundation Award for being the most effective charity operating in Canada, compared to a cross section of over 600 other charities doing similar work. With this ongoing success, I began to research why this type of program is so effective in treating women and girls who have faced such deep trauma and horrors in life.

Little research has actually been done into evaluating the Post-Traumatic Stress Disorders that can arise in women from experiencing violence, rape, ongoing sexual assaults, or domestic beatings. The existing research shows that women and girls do very well in PTSD recovery and management when they participate in experiential life skills classes, which is exactly what we were doing at our charity. Thus, began my most recent work: to educate people on the differences in women's and children's PTSD cycles arising from ongoing abuses and violence, as contrasted to the PTSD of military survival. Neither is worse than the other. The brain, however, reacts differently to each experience, and we must continue to study the effectiveness of experiential courses for women and girls and boys overcoming their PTSD.

Today, I continue to have the kind of relationships I deserve. They nurture me and give me balance and good health. My life is not without sadness, loneliness, or grief; however, I have the tools and the gratitude to embrace the bad and ugly with the good. I am a fulfilled, loved, and content woman. I am a whole and complete woman of worth and value, no matter what.

Remember: you are the center of all your relationships, therefore you are responsible for your self-esteem, growth, happiness, and fulfillment. Don't expect the other people in your life to bring you these things.

About Mary Pichette

Mary Pichette is the only individual in Canada who is certified by Life Skills Training Centres Canada Ltd. as a Master Trainer of Life Skills Coaches. This represents a seven-year study of group process and a three-year residency in conducting Life Skills Training Groups.

Mary has trained over 400 Life Skills Coaches, Family Management Counsellors, and Human Relations Group Facilitators. She has worked with over 2000 individuals, teaching them skills in how to have healthy relationships and how to effectively solve their people problems. She is highly regarded for her training, speaking, and seminars. Past students are highly satisfied with her skills as a trainer and have had very successful outcomes in their own lives as a result of the training they received.

Mary has taught criminology at colleges and universities in BC and Alberta, opened some of the first transition houses in Canada, and trained the first volunteers in Canada to work sexual assault crisis lines. As Executive Director of Servants Anonymous Society, she responded very effectively to the first calls for help for highly publicized cases of rescued human trafficking victims from across Canada. Today, Mary is asked to consult and speak to the issues surrounding:

- Post-Traumatic Stress Disorder in women
- Experiential learning and its relevance to recovery from mental illness in women
- Life Skills Coach Training
- Creating, nurturing and sustaining whole and healthy relationships
- How to relate effectively in every personal interaction
- How to effectively solve Interpersonal problems leading to improved relationships
- Human trafficking across Canada and Western U.S.
- First Nations learning outcomes

www.marypichette.com
Email: info@marypichette.com
Twitter: @marypichette
Instagram: Askpichette

6

THE GENIUS OF ADHD

by Lee-Ann Davenport

"Imperfection is beauty, madness is genius, and it's better to be absolutely ridiculous than to be boring."
Unknown

The Genius of ADHD

by Lee-Ann Davenport

Isn't it interesting how life takes us down such a mysterious path to what we become? Do you ever wonder where you'd be today if just one thing was different? I've considered myself pretty lucky for most of my life, but now I've realized that none of it was luck. We spend a lifetime developing self-awareness and finding ways to better ourselves, but it's not just our behaviors that need improvement; it goes far beyond that. It's our brain that we need to educate ourselves about. With today's imaging technology there is a lot of new information on how the human mind works, and we're only just scratching the surface.

It wasn't until our son was clinically diagnosed at the age of ten, when I was forty-nine, that I finally learned the full meaning of ADHD: Attention Deficit Hyperactivity Disorder. It's quite astonishing that so many people, like me, know these words but haven't a clue as to what they mean. I was in complete disbelief, because I am also ADHD and never knew it! This incredibly invaluable piece of information would have made a world of a difference in my life. Not that it would have changed anything about me, but it would have helped me explain my behaviors, good and bad, to those who've been impacted by them.

Let me tell you this: ADHD is not a disability, it is a different ability. What I have is not an actual disorder or mental illness. Neither my son, nor I, have learning disabilities, and by definition a disorder is an illness and I am NOT sick. Therefore, the words ADHD don't make logical sense. We (ADHDers) may have behavioral problems, but we are not ill – we are different. We may suffer and struggle, but that's because society, for the most part, is not accepting of our differences and can be quite judgmental.

My brain does not typically think the "normal" way. One author, Peter Shankman, has written a book for people with ADHD called "Faster Than Normal." He states that because we're keen observers and process many ideas simultaneously with minimal effort, we're great conversationalists, can improvise on the fly, may have sharp wit, can instantly assimilate new information into previous knowledge to create original insights, are inspired by change, have an ability to find quick solutions to complex situations, think laterally (and in curvilinear ways as opposed to linear), and so on. I certainly relate to all of that! He goes on to say, "if we don't harness these gifts, we'll go crashing into a concrete wall at 600 mph, every single time."

It is my hope that readers open their minds to a new perspective, without letting their opinions get in the way, in order to understand that the complexity of ADHD goes far beyond what I am describing on many different levels. It is my wish to inspire those with ADHD and those who *might* have it, and to encourage those who don't to be supportive of those who do. Success for us is merely a quest to be accepted and loved, just like everyone else.

I grew up in a family of six. There was my mom and dad, my sister, and two brothers. I was the oldest, with rest of us one year apart in age. Yes, our mom had her hands full, especially as all of us had ADD/ADHD! We were a family just like everyone else's, or so I thought. I could see that every family had their own set of dysfunctions just like ours, but I grew up knowing something was quite different about us. Was it because we were from Quebec? Who knows, but we were the only Creviers in the phone book in the greater Vancouver area for a long time.

Instead of trying to describe our family, I put the question out on social media and these were the first responses:

"Crazy, fun, wild, loud, and louder. Generous, athletic, and did I say fun?"
"Loving, accepting, fun, wild, crazy family…"
"Fun-loving, fearless, and slightly reckless."

Notice the theme. Yes, nothing short of entertainment when you put us all in a room together!

While everyone in my family played hockey (mom and sister included), I was a gymnast. I loved ballet and went into competitive gymnastics, training for four hours a day every day after school. The gym was my life, and it was this discipline that was to shape my future.

Throughout high school I struggled with trying to understand the question of "what do I want to be when I grow up?" I loved school and it was always super easy for me, but because I didn't have any idea of what to take, I decided not to go to university. Instead, I thought that I'd figure it out by just getting out into the working world. Little did I know the value of a degree!

I was very fortunate to have grown up with a lot of freedom to do as I pleased. There was always support from my parents with any of my choices and never any negativity or dictation of what I could or couldn't do. As a result, I was one to always question everything. I used to believe what I had was common sense, but it's actually intuition – my "inner wisdom." For example, my thoughts on getting married were, "could I live with this man for the rest of my life?" Even though I was in love and engaged at eighteen, I still asked myself this question. But the universe drew me away, so I didn't need to find out that answer.

When I was twenty, everything in my life changed. I became a certified aerobics instructor, and when I landed my first job teaching I knew I had found my calling and my greatest joy in life! Instantly, I declared that this is what I'll be doing until I'm eighty. I taught my first class like a pro as it felt so natural to me. I never had to plan, rehearse, or practice prior to teaching any class; it all came to me the minute I started the music and let my body fuel my brain. I was able to spontaneously create a class packed with fun and challenge to keep people addicted for more. My passion for teaching is still just as powerful now as it was then, and the gift of being ADHD contributes to the energy and attitude that enables me to just know what to do.

For several years, I was working many part and full-time jobs while always teaching somewhere. I was constantly on the go, working and living in many different places. As I jumped from job to job, I used to wonder why I could never stay in one place for very long. One thing for sure is that working at fitness clubs and restaurants or bars was a lot of fun! To this day, I love the night life. Dancing, loud music, and being social is my "happy place." Chalk that up to being ADHD.

Around this time, I started to notice that I had these unexplainable behaviours that, at times, made people angry. When this happened, I couldn't understand why people were upset, especially since I would never intentionally do anything to disappoint or hurt them. While I was being spontaneous and perhaps naïve, people would perceive me as being inconsiderate because my actions weren't making sense. For example, one Saturday I suddenly decided to go to my family's place at Whistler to go skiing. My boyfriend was working late and didn't ski, so I went on my own. The problem was that it was Valentine's Day. My boyfriend was not happy that I disappeared without mentioning anything, but for some reason the importance of this day didn't occur to me. Perhaps it was because the year before I was alone, so I had to remove any relevance from that day. With ADHD, sometimes the short-term memory is nonexistent and the long-term memory overrides current situations and thoughts. Even today, I forget that I might need to consider communicating my whereabouts or plans to my husband. If I'm busy concentrating on work, out shopping, or with people, I'm purely living in the present moment.

I could keep writing about more stories of so many more ADHD problems like distractions, time management, hyperfocusing, hypersensitivity, and more, and how I found ways to turn some of these negative traits into positive ones, like using reverse psychology to overcome obstacles and working with my creativity to find solutions. Perhaps in a future book!

One might say that becoming an entrepreneur is a great accomplishment. For me, it wasn't an accomplishment, but a decision. For three years I knew I wanted to own a business, but at what? I had no idea, until one day I was reading an American fitness magazine and there is it was: a full-page advertisement on the First Annual One-to-One Personal Fitness Trainers Conference in Los Angeles. It was March of 1989, and I lit up like a firecracker. This was it! I instantly booked myself to go and started my company, LA Lifestyles Health & Fitness Consulting – LA as in my nickname, not the city, by the way. A month later I was off to gain the best education ever. Intuition and spontaneity at its best!

The whole experience was an affirmation that I already had what it takes to be a trainer. I was more than just confident; I was ready. I was savvy in creating ways to build clientele without spending money and, like magic, my energy created the Ripple Effect and the Laws of Attraction were all aligning. My modest year-end goal was to be training ten clients two to three times per week, but I more than exceeded that. I ended up with twelve clients, of which the last two were partners in an architect firm of ninety employees. They hired me to create an employee fitness program, train all thirteen executive managers, teach fitness classes for the employees five days a week, promote other activities, and book fitness testing to motivate those interested in pursuing more fitness in their lives. I had my hands full, and I was loving every minute of it. This was all before anyone even knew what personal training was. There were no certifications or courses of any kind, and people thought only movie stars had personal trainers. This was not a career to plan for or a job to get hired at; it barely existed in Canada. But none of that mattered because I had a vision. At the age of twenty-six, I was living my entrepreneurial dream, with no plan, me just being me, unconventional and ADHD.

Over the next five years I had many ups and downs, from doing financially well to scraping rock bottom. I ran a few different corporate fitness programs, only to realize that this was not the direction for me. I also decided I needed to stop the madness of driving all over town from gyms to homes, so I rented a studio space, quit teaching classes, and started buying my own fitness equipment. But I still needed more focus and zeroed in on a way to expand without having to hire trainers. I found the solution when a friend encouraged me to purchase an artist live/work studio, so my first husband and I bought one together.

The decision made perfect sense. It was a smart move to invest into real estate and establish an exclusive private training studio, and we were paying less for a mortgage than it cost to rent two places. Unfortunately, this wasn't ideal for my husband and our marriage ended. In moving forward, I found a new love who was perfect in supporting me and my business. Once again, my vision became a reality and business became very successful. Everything was going great but boredom was settling in; not with the work itself, but with the "routine." Just another ADHD phase!

After five great years of living and working in my studio loft space, one day I turned to my boyfriend of four years and said, "I need to make a new five-year business plan. Or, do we want to make a family plan?" He had always wanted kids, and suddenly at the age of thirty-six, I was ready – a bit bizarre, as I grew up never wanting to have children.

Daniel was born when I was thirty-eight, and it was such a beautiful gift to finally become a mother. Everything fell into place, of course: we sold the loft, moved the gym to a new location, moved into a house, and got married two years later, all within the exact timeline I had anticipated. In 2007, when Daniel was six years old, we made a spontaneous decision to move to the Okanagan, which started a whole new chapter in my life.

Motherhood. Where do I begin? They say it's harder for girls to have ADHD than boys, but it's even harder for women to be ADHD and mothers, too. In addition, the inevitable marriage problems were escalating, business was inconsistent, and I couldn't get my life together. I floated in and out of depression, which was often severe, and my behavior continued to be the problem for my husband as it was driving him crazy. Until that fateful day when we learned about ADHD. To me, this was a godsend! It was the missing link that was never brought to light. I had learned a lot over the years about myself from psychology books, a self-development course, career counselling, and personality testing. I've also hired two business coaches, neither of whom reached the goals I had in mind. I kept wondering why I couldn't get ahead and what was wrong with this situation. Never once in this time did I come across any information on ADHD.

I now know that a set program doesn't usually work for me, so how can it work for the thousands like me? Just imagine if a personal trainer put you on a set program, and you had to stick to it with no consideration for your personal needs. Professionals are missing the mark in creating success for countless ADHDers. The school system isn't working in our favour either, yet society still expects the "square to fit into the circle." It is quite mind boggling, as we have brilliant minds!

Despite all my hurdles, I am blessed with my abilities, including being stubborn, determined, and defiant. When I struggled to rebuild my business in the tough economic times in my small town of Lake Country, BC, I dug deep into my soul to find a new career. I soon built up the courage to create a business in the interior design field and painting industry, even though I had zero credentials and little experience. I knew I had the innate talents for interior design as it has been a long-time passion, and I learned how fun painting was when I filled all four of my homes with expressive colours. By 2011,

I had developed LA Home Staging Painting + Design and rediscovered a new me; the hidden talents, the therapy of painting, and the success from being a perfectionist.

Along with letting go of pursuing personal training, I also found a new love and inspiration in yoga. This practice is miraculous in healing body, mind, and spirit. As active as I am, my injuries and my age have caught up with me; as a result, I suffer from chronic low back pain. I have been transitioning slowly in the past year, planning to take myself to another level as an entrepreneur. I am determined to rise above my battles of pain, both physically and mentally, to achieve even more than I can imagine. Because planning for the future isn't quite in my "know-how," my goal is to reinvent myself again and to continue to recreate ways to teach. I am thrilled that I have found my niche in Somatic Yoga, which is a type of movement therapy, and that this will take me to living life pain-free physically, mentally, and spiritually. It is my greatest reward to bring better health and happiness to people, because making you happy ultimately makes me happy!

Throughout my life I have learned many lessons, and some of them have become ingenious rules to live by:

Embrace Being Different

Own being who you are, with all the imperfections you have. Be proud and love feeling alive! By being present and lit up within, you have the right to feel happy at ALL times. Allow no one to dim that light and remain grateful for all that you are. Not everyone will understand you, so be selective about who you want to share your stories with. You deserve full support!

Apologize Graciously

We all screw up from time to time. Recognize any behaviors you have that may make someone feel uncomfortable or surprised and make an apology, not to claim fault but to acknowledge the others' situation. For example, "I'm sorry, I didn't mean to be rude by interrupting. I am impulsive at times and just can't contain my excitement!" By showing consideration, you are expressing compassion as opposed to what may first be perceived as being self-centered. You deserve forgiveness.

You Never Get a Second Chance at a First Impression

Remember to try to think first before speaking. If you are in an environment with unfamiliar people, you may want to show respect and earn silent positive praise, first by actively listening and greeting with eye contact. A simple "hello" with a warm smile just may be enough to invite a conversation. Your beaming aura has already made an impression, and by being patient your turn to take the stage will happen. You deserve love.

If by chance you do or say something "wrong," remember that it's not wrong as we know it, but different. Then, go back to the first two rules. While these are important tools for ADHDers, they are equally valuable for everyone else too!

Embracing my ADHD has given me the opportunity to learn so much more about myself and do things that would otherwise be impossible. I hope this chapter has given you the opportunity to see the world from a new perspective and embrace your own differences. Now go and find your support, your tribe, and your sisters, and lead with clarity!

"No matter what your current circumstances, if you can imagine something better for yourself, you can create it."
John Assaraf

About Lee-Ann Davenport

Lee-Ann Davenport – owner, visionary, serial entrepreneur, and now author and speaker – currently operates two companies in separate industries.

LA Home Staging Painting + Design was developed in 2011 when Lee-Ann decided to pursue a dream job in the field of interior design as a home stager and by also entering the market as an interior painter. Lee-Ann's attention to detail and an "eye for design" is what makes her stand out. Her success as a stager, interior stylist, colour consultant, and painter is built from a reputation that exceeds client expectations.

LA Lifestyles was originally a personal fitness training business which Lee-Ann started in 1989 as she pioneered through an unknown career at the time. She has just recently rebranded and is transitioning her company to specialize in teaching Somatic Yoga along with private training for people who live with pain and other health ailments. Her approach to health and wellness is backed by thirty-five years of experience in the health and fitness industry and has renewed her passion for teaching people who value having an active lifestyle, a strong body and mind, and living well in balance and harmony.

New to her repertoire of becoming an author and speaker, Lee-Ann is an advocate on ADHD, pain management, and somatics. She believes it is vitally important to inform, educate, and empower women, and has made it her mission to teach people how to advocate for themselves and be experts on their own minds and bodies. We are unique individuals who can make a difference in achieving the ultimate goal in life: happiness!

www.lalifestyles.ca
www.lahome.ca
Facebook: L A Lifestyles Health & Fitness Consulting
Facebook: L A Home Staging Painting + Design

7

THE CREATIVE ENTREPRENEUR

by Diane Lund

"Whatever you can do or dream you can,
Begin it.
Boldness has genius, power and magic in it."
Goethe

The Creative Entrepreneur

by Diane Lund

I never wanted to be an entrepreneur; all I ever wanted to be was creative. When I was taking English and Communications as a double major at university with the intention to move towards my goal of spending a lifetime being creative, I made two big promises to myself. The first was that I did not want to be a business owner like my Dad, because it looked too hard. The second was that I did not want to be a starving artist.

My parents had grown up during the Depression, and they had many stories of going hungry and foraging in the forest or along the ocean's edge for food. They ate oysters, dandelion greens, and forest mushrooms. Today these foods might be considered delicacies, but back then it was just plain survival. I knew I did not want to simply survive; I wanted to *thrive*, and I wanted to do it by being creative and helping others. So, I decided I would be a writer.

At Simon Fraser University, I applied to work with a

famous playwright and I got the job as her writing partner. We worked together, along with a group of actors, to create a play that they would one day perform. It was hard work. The playwright was demanding, temperamental, and exhausting; it was simply one drama after the next. But, I persevered and eventually a play emerged called "Tracings: The Simon Fraser Story," which went on to be filmed and shown on CBC. With this play-writing experience and an honours arts degree under my belt, I decided it was time to apply for my first job as a writer.

Everyone said, "That's a joke. There are no jobs for writers out there." I was determined, though, that I was going to succeed. All I had to do was find the elusive paid writer's job.

It's Your Fortunate Day Cookie

After graduating I took a job as a receptionist for immediate cash flow, and then I set my mind to find somewhere I could work as a writer. After an exhaustive search of companies in Vancouver I decided I wanted to work for Creative House, which wrote and produced large slide shows for corporate companies like Air Canada. At the time, they worked in the industrial section of downtown, which was filled with old brick buildings and small creative firms. I told my Dad my plan. He thought I was crazy and wasn't afraid to tell me so, but I would not be shaken or pulled off course. I asked him if I could come to his office and use some of his supplies to put a project together and he agreed, so off I went to make my special resume. When I finished, he promptly looked at it and announced, "That will never get you a job." So much for positive encouragement!

The next day, I put my plan into action. I had purchased a bunch of fortune cookies and put specific messages in each cookie. Then I had a courier deliver the cookies one by one to the owner of Creative House. The first cookie said something like, "Today will be a day you will never forget." The next cookie said, "Soon you will meet a woman that will change your life." The last cookie was the one I had made at my Dad's office. It was made out of a bendable plastic that I had shaped into the form of a fortune cookie, and I had put transfer letters on the top which read "It's Your Fortunate Day Cookie!" I had placed my resume inside the plastic cookie. About ten minutes after the final cookie was delivered, I received a phone call from the owner. He said he had to meet me and to come see him immediately, even though it was after 5:00 PM. I raced to his office.

After an enthusiastic greeting, the owner asked me if I knew what I had just done. I told him I thought I had asked for a job, but he informed me that I'd done much more than that. He told me, "What you did today is called a marketing plan. You decided on a goal, you created a strategy to achieve that goal, and then you implemented it. That's what you did today in order to get a job, and guess what?"

"What?" I asked, waiting with bated breath.

"I do NOT have a job."

"Oh no," I said. "Many people told me you would not have a job for me, but I did not want to believe them."

"Well, that's a great thing because although I do NOT have a job for you, I am willing to MAKE a job for you. I haven't seen this kind of creativity in a long time and I don't want to let it pass me by. You can start on Monday." And with that statement, my professional writing career began. The doubters had been wrong. I had believed in myself and my dream, and now it was all coming true. I was ecstatic.

The Long and Short Of It

Writing was never easy for me because there is no definite "right and wrong." Whether someone liked my writing or did not like my writing was often subjective, and as a result the work was often frustrating.

After a year at Creative House, I decided I did not want to work on big long assignments. I was young and wanted to move from project to project much faster, as I thought this might cut down on the frustration I was feeling.

I surprised myself by deciding I wanted to work in advertising. From the outside, it looked like I could still be creative but the projects were shorter. Radio and television commercials were just thirty or sixty seconds, very different from the thirty-minute or hour-long programs I currently worked on which took months to produce. So, I started the search for my next perfect job.

My Next Ad-venture!

It took much longer to land a job in the field of advertising, but eventually I was hired as a writer/producer at a downtown agency. I was thrilled! I loved the variety of work, and I quickly started to write and produce weekly broadcast campaigns for Canada Safeway.

What a fabulous learning period this was for me. Over a six-year period I would bring all of Canada Safeway's radio and television ads under one large marketing campaign in British Columbia, Alberta, Saskatoon, Manitoba, and Ontario. It was an amazing accomplishment because each province had been doing their own thing, and so uniting the company's advertising under one creative campaign helped them create a stronger national brand while also saving the company money. But for years I was working around the clock for people that worked in head offices far away, and the hard work took its toll. Over time I realized there was a lack of personal connection and meaning; for me, that was critical. I had always been fascinated with spirituality and I could see that I was moving away from my inner spirit needs to satisfy my outer physical needs. As I was extremely busy, it was easy to ignore these inner feelings. However, after a decade of hard work I realized that I felt a serious void in my life; a vital lack of meaning in just putting out ad after ad that talked about the "price of things." There must be more to life! My excitement with my job was waning, and all the late nights and busy days left my personal relationships wanting more of me too. Something had to change.

The Writing is On the Wall

I decided I needed to find a job that had something more meaningful to offer to the world. Personally, I was interested in spirituality, alternative health, and the environment. So, when I had heard about a production company that was in town producing shows on alternative health, the environment, and metaphysics, I naturally thought, "This is my next step. I need to apply my writing and production skills to topics I am really interested in." I prayed, "If I am meant to work for this new U.S. production company that is in town, I need their card by the end of this week." Low and behold, the next day someone handed me the business card of the Production Company's producer. Wow, that was fast!

I was convinced I had to jump on this opportunity, so I decided I would do another "marketing campaign for myself." This time, I got a good bottle of wine, soaked off the label, and made a new one. I wrote on it: "A fine, bold WHINE: I want to work for you!" Of course, the campaign was successful and I went to work for this television company.

I have to admit, working on television shows that focused on my personal areas of interest was wonderful. I travelled to the United States with Canadian stars, and I got to talk on local radio stations about subjects that I was truly interested in marketing and promoting. What I was doing had a real purpose. However, there was a serious flaw that was soon to be revealed.

The Dream Goes South

Turns out, a company in the States was raising capital to fund the shows I was working on. Someone in the investment company decided to reroute the investment dollars raised through his personal bank account, and he got caught by U.S. regulation authorities. All the money had to go back to the investors, and the man - who said he was just using the money to get a mortgage and had intended to return it - went to jail. Suddenly, everyone lost his or her job. It was shocking for the whole company, but not to me. Here's why.

I had been having doubts about my relationships as well as doubts about my career. It seemed that just switching jobs or switching boyfriends did not make me happy. Because of this, I had sought out a counsellor whose work was truly beginning to transform my life. I started off by going to one of his talks, then one of his sessions, then to his workshops, and slowly over time I was sold.

I decided I had spent too much time pursuing career goals and not enough time pursing personal goals. I knew I needed to work on my life and myself at a place called The Haven where this counsellor gave his workshops. So, for over a month I had been asking my boss if I could take the time to go to a month-long course at The Haven in the fall. My boss had told me, "There is no way you are going. We are just too busy!" But that afternoon he called me into the office and said, "I guess you were right. You will be going to that month-long program, because you no longer have a job!"

You know what they say: when one door closes, a window opens. Losing my job and going to The Haven was the opening I needed to truly change in my life. I went to Phase One, where you live on the property and go to personal growth workshops all day and through the evening.

The first phase program was about exploring self, and it was beyond amazing. Through breath work, Reiki, acupuncture, bodywork, and other techniques, I started to dig into my past and see where my alcoholic family had left their wounds. I felt a fire in myself to look within. The experience was so exciting and transformative that I took all four phases, and after a year I decided to take their Diploma of Counselling. Perhaps I needed to be a counsellor and not a writer. But, whatever I was going to do, I still needed to pay my bills.

Putting Heart Into Art

I had a small amount of savings, but that was quickly running out as I was taking programs and not working. When people started to ask me to help them market their projects, I told them, "I am training to be a counsellor, I have left the writing and producing behind." But people were persistent. They knew of my past and they wanted help. Eventually, with a lot of badgering, I decided I would help those folks whose projects I had "heart" for. So, on the side, I started to help people. My first creative project was to help "struggling and starving artists." Ironic, you might say.

The problem with many artists is they love to make their art, but they do not know how to market their art and do not have the money for traditional media. So, I solved the problem by creating a TV show and magazine called Arts Access, where they could feature their projects and talk to their audiences. I was helping artists not starve, and it felt good! Both ventures were a success. Eventually more people heard about what I was doing, and before long I was writing and producing almost full time again. This time, though, I was working for myself. I still did not want a company, so I told myself I was just doing something I enjoyed. However, I discovered this line of thinking is kind of like having sex and enjoying it without thinking about the baby that will be born from your *fun*. Over time, I slowly began to realize I had birthed a whole new company, but I was reluctant to admit what was happening. People were asking me, "Don't you have a business card? What is your company's name?" I had neither. Finally, I had to bite the bullet and admit the baby was here and it was time to take responsibility.

Creative Wonders Communications Now Twenty-Five Years Strong!

I called my new baby Creative Wonders Communications, and I was determined that this time I was going to do advertising and marketing from a whole different place. I was not going to locate my company downtown, but in my community on Vancouver's North Shore instead. I was also going to focus on areas I loved: the environment and recycling, alternative health, community, and creativity.

My friends were appalled. Remember, this was in a time before the Internet. Today you can work and connect from just about anywhere, but back then people thought you needed to all be together in an office downtown to be connected. They told me, "You are running away." I knew, though, that this was not true. I was forging my own path.

Today, just about everyone recycles their home newspapers, cardboard, glass jars, tin cans, and even their compost materials. Many people are now interested in the environment and sustainability, but this was the beginning of the 1990's and it was going to take about twenty years for these topics to become household names and common ways of being. I wanted to be a part of changing and supporting my community and doing what I loved. Little did I know that this new emerging market had a name: L.O.H.A.S., an acronym that stands for "Lifestyles of Health and Sustainability." Who knew? I was just following my heart.

Growing up, I never wanted a company, and I never wanted to be an entrepreneur; all I wanted was to work creatively doing something that helped people. When I look back now, I can see that this is exactly what happened. In fact, my company positioning line for years was "going beyond making a living to making a difference!"

This year, I celebrate twenty-five years of being the owner and Creative Director of Creative Wonders Communications. Over the years, I have had the distinct pleasure of helping hundreds of local, regional, and national companies achieve their creative and professional goals. In addition, I have employed over fifty people and helped them pursue their life dreams. Some highlights of my entrepreneurial life include winning many awards; not just for creativity but also for entrepreneurship, innovation, and giving back to my community.

Today, my advice to all entrepreneurs is you do not have to know where you are going, just follow your heart and listen to your inner intuition. Your gut knows! Trust the divine working in your life, and do not believe the doubters. Do not be afraid to think out of the box and be creative; who knows the good you might do! Also, hire an excellent bookkeeper, because money is important. It is the fuel behind getting things done.

And finally: yes, the world does need your special blend of creativity and genius! Believe in yourself, and see how magical your life can truly become.

About Diane C. Lund

A thirty-five-year veteran of the advertising, communication, and marketing business, Diane works directly with clients to determine their vision, objectives, and desired results. She then writes up the marketing strategy and her team helps her produce stellar creative projects for both traditional and digital media. No matter whether your business is local or global, small or big, retail or corporate, Diane has the experience and depth to lead the way.

Diane has won many awards for her work, including the International Silver Summit Award for Online Marketing Effectiveness, the Visioneers International Network Lifetime Achievement Award for Innovation and Entrepreneurship, Ethics In Action for Community Care, and the Best Business Award from the Chamber of Commerce Business Excellence Awards.

Ever pursuing her creative and spiritual side, Diane recently became a Reverend focused on A Course in Miracles with CIMM – Canadian International Metaphysical Ministries. Her new book, "Turn Your World Upside Down To Get Your Life Right Side Up: Reverse Thinking Based On A Course In Miracles," and the accompanying e-workbook, "SOULutions: Putting Reverse Thinking Into Day-to-Day Practise," will be out in 2018.

Receive a free e-book titled "Ready, Aim, Fire: The Keys To Unlocking Business Creativity," and listen to a free webinar titled "The 10 A's for Awesome Marketing Success" on her Creative Wonders website.

www.creativewonders.ca
www.dianelundmiracles.ca
Facebook: Creative Wonders Communications Inc.
Twitter: creativewonders
LinkedIn: dianelund
Email: diane@creativewonders.ca

8

THE SWEET SIDE OF DEPRESSION

by Trish Tansley

"THE 3 C'S OF LIFE:
CHOICES, CHANCES & CHANGE
You MUST make a CHOICE to take a CHANCE
or your life will never CHANGE!"
Trish Tansley

The Sweet Side of Depression

by Trish Tansley

Most people that meet me have no idea that I was raised on a sheep ranch and lived the ranch life until my mid-twenties. Our ranch was in Moses Lake, Washington, along with about 1000 acres of farmland where we grew wheat and alfalfa. This meant that we were not only taking care of the livestock every day, but also changing the irrigation usually both before and after school.

I had a good childhood – we worked very hard to make sure everything got done, but we played hard as well. My parents always did fun stuff with us and we traveled as much as possible. I will always admire my mom and dad for the life that they gave me, and I give so much credit to them as they are the reason I have such a strong work ethic. Because of my upbringing, I have always been able to "power through" any situation that has been thrown in front of me.

On May 18, 1980, Mount Saint Helens erupted. The next

day we saw the devastation and destruction, and all I could think was "what's left?" About two years later, we lost the ranch and my dad started working for other ranches; even at the age of sixteen, it was hard to watch him go from owning his own ranch to working for others. This gave me a certain perspective on entrepreneurship and being in control. It wasn't until I was in Corporate America in my late twenties that I realized I had an entrepreneurial mindset like my parents. It took me until my mid to late thirties to finally say that I had enough of working for corporations! I truly wanted to get off the hamster wheel and be done with working for someone else.

Between 2000 and 2013, I created and operated nine different businesses. Some of them were successful and some of them just did okay, but most just didn't stick. That being said, I learned something valuable from each of them.

In 2004 I married a Canadian and moved to Fort McMurray, Alberta. Here I found ways to create businesses through my husband's name as I wasn't supposed to be working; it took three years for my first visa to come through and six years to get my Permanent Residency. Seven months after that, we divorced.

Soon after, I moved to Cochrane, Alberta, and I was building my new life. I was running my homemade gourmet treat business while working independently as a Health Care Aide, and I had a great opportunity with the Town of Cochrane. A couple years later, I had moved into a new condo, I had a new boyfriend (Scott), and I was loving the life I was creating! In 2013 I was offered an opportunity to work as a Property Manager in Airdrie, Alberta, and it was a no brainer to accept the role. The hours were good, the pay was great, and I could eventually work from home – almost like being an entrepreneur in one of my own businesses!

The Day That Changed my Life

Unbeknownst to me, my world would soon completely change. About six weeks into my new job as a Property Manager, I was driving through an intersection on my way to work when a Ford Escape turned in front of me and I plowed into them with my Jeep Grand Cherokee. I literally saw a white flash to the left side of me and that was it; I had been knocked out momentarily. As I walked by my vehicle, I was shocked to find that the front was almost completely squished in. Both cars were a total loss. Scott took me to the hospital as he said I just wasn't acting right. I remember beginning to feel uneasy as I was sitting in the waiting room, so I walked over to the nurse's station. They told me it wouldn't be long and to let them know if things got worse. On the way back I remember feeling lethargic, and then nothing; I've been told that I passed out face first on the floor. When I came to, I had been placed in a room.

The next day I woke up and could barely move; I was in serious pain and stuck on the couch. Three days later I saw my family Doctor and she commented how I was acting different, although I didn't fully understand what she meant. She assessed my injuries and stated that it would be best for me to see a Physiotherapist as soon as possible.

Now, as a workaholic, all I could think about was my job! I had finally found something that I really liked to do, and it came with a lot of perks. What was I going to do? How could I cover up the pain? I rested on the couch all day Monday, but Tuesday was a different story. Even though I knew that my injuries were becoming very serious, I felt that I needed to figure out a way to work no matter what.

I was managing just fine, or at least that's what I told myself.

I was in a lot of non-stop pain, but I sat at the kitchen table working on my laptop. My parents had taught me to "power through" any situation that was put in front of me, but they didn't prepare me for this – who could?

Two weeks after my accident, I was let go.

A month and a half after the accident, Scott was offered a job in British Columbia. There was nothing keeping us in Cochrane any longer, so we decided to make the move and we arrived in Langley in the summer of 2013. Due to the extent of my pain, I was lucky to find a family doctor who was willing to take me on as a patient in my first week there, although Scott had to call six different clinics to find one. After six months of excruciating physio, sleep deprivation, constant headaches, and just down right hopelessness, my doctor referred me to a Physiatrist due to my lack of progress. Finally! The Physiatrist was able to diagnose me with Chronic Mylo Fascia (chronic muscle damage) and a mild brain injury. Although the news wasn't rosy, having a label for my condition gave me a sense of sanity and a new direction for how to address my symptoms.

For two full years after the accident, I sat on the couch depressed and feeling sorry for myself because I couldn't do much. I was in a deep depression with no signs of motivation, and the only thing that made me happy was eating sweets. Instead of that beaming smile, creative spark, and "walk in the room" energy that I used to have before my accident, I looked dull and tired, I was always moody, and I felt terrible most of the time.

One evening, the thought of my life and the pain I was feeling became overwhelming. Scott found me sitting on the couch, looking as lifeless as a living human body could be. He came over, sat next to me, and tried to get me to talk, but I couldn't. No words would come out – there was no sign of anything in my eyes except a blank gaze. I didn't even feel like I was in my body anymore. How could I explain to him what I was feeling? When he decided to shake me lightly, I seemed to come out of my trance. He said, "I am seriously worried. What is going on? What is wrong?" When I answered, I remember feeling the words fall out of my mouth without a thought to what I had actually said. "I just can't take the pain anymore, I don't know how to deal with this on a daily basis, I am not getting better, and nothing is helping!" He replied, "Time, it's just going to take time, you will get better." I remember feeling very dull and saying, "You always say that and here it is, two years later! I can't put on a happy face anymore to cover it up. I don't want you in my life, I don't want to be here anymore…I'm just done." Scott then said, "I just don't know how to help you anymore, maybe we could find someone to help you." I knew then that I had just hit my lowest point of my life. Something had to change.

Making a Choice, Taking a Chance

"Through our greatest pain and our darkest times
can we truly appreciate & discover our true selves."
Unknown

We started researching Psychologists the very next day and found one that deals directly with post traumatic stress disorder and chronic pain management from motor vehicle accidents. I worked with this Psychologist for three months, and it was hard! I cried in almost every session, re-living the accident and the last two years of my life, but I knew that this was a crucial step in breaking through my trauma to understand and become aware of what was feeding my deep depression. In three months, she was able to teach me coping mechanisms to manage my chronic pain and to help me accept that I would have to live with this for the rest of my life and learn to move forward.

I also learned that I was using sugar to cover up my pain, and as far as anyone knew it was working. I thought had everyone fooled, until I put on thirty pounds and found myself wondering how this had happened.

I needed a change and had too many bad memories in Langley, so we decided to move to White Rock. After we settled in I took on a few small contracting jobs, but I still found that I wasn't fulfilled or happy. I knew that it wasn't what I really wanted to do long-term, and based on my current physical condition I knew I had to make even more changes. I decided that I wanted to change my eating habits and learn how to stop using sugar to numb my chronic pain and depression. I found a local Nutritionist and decided to take a twenty-eight-day whole foods body reset; Scott, being the supportive partner that he is, decided to take this program with me. I'm so glad that he did as it was super hard to change the way that I had been eating for over two years. During this body reset, I finally figured out and admitted that I was a Sugar Addict! I had found the "sweet side" of my depression, and this is where my life completely changed. I was finally starting to feel like myself again.

I did a 180 on my eating habits, I developed skills to cope with my chronic pain, my lifestyle had improved, and I had a new outlook on what I wanted to do for my future. I was told by my Nutritionist and people around me that I had a natural ability to talk with people. While this can mean a lot of things, it made me think deeper about what I could do for long-term that would be sustainable both emotionally and physically.

This led me on a path to research just the right program for exactly what I wanted to do, and after six months of research I discovered a program to be trained as a Holistic Health Coach. It encompassed everything that I could imagine wanting to learn about how to guide other people in creating holistic, sustainable, healthy lifestyles.

After six months of intensive training, I was super excited to begin my new career! I had a fresh outlook on life and I was now certified to help others looking to change their habits, struggling with food addictions, and feeling like they are stuck in a rut. I knew that I could help these people, because I'd been there and been through it myself. So, for my thirteenth (and hopefully last) business, I started Holistic Healthy Habits. Now, this didn't happen overnight; it took a bit of time to create programs and figure out the who, what, and how of what I was doing. My knowledge of business and education took me through most of the process, but then I hit a rut, as a lot of entrepreneurs do, and I didn't know how to move forward. I had a plan for how everything was supposed to go, but I wasn't able to follow through with it. I needed to figure out how to move past this, just as I did everything else in my life. I knew I was going to succeed. This was my passion, and I was determined to make it work! I had to figure out what was holding me back. Or let me put it differently, I knew "what" was holding me back, I just didn't know how to move past it.

Despite being stuck, I refused to look for advice on what I should do. It wasn't about being in control, it was about asking for help – something I was never taught to do.

Enough is Enough

About four months later, the lightbulb switched on and I finally figured it out: there was nothing wrong with my business, *I* was the problem! As an entrepreneur, this was incredibly hard to admit. It wasn't that I didn't have time to figure out what the next step in my business was, but that I didn't have time to work on me. Yes, me! I still needed to come to grips with the reality that I cannot work a regular job, as holding onto this mentality was keeping me from moving forward. I finally figured out that I was always trying to do it all, and I wouldn't – or didn't know how to – ask for help. I had heard of other entrepreneurs getting a coach or mentor, but I thought I didn't need any assistance.

Finally, I pulled the plug and I, Trish Tansley, asked for help and hired a coach! It went against everything that I had grown up to believe, but I did it. This coach had nothing to do with my sugar addiction or my emotional and physical pain; she solely focused on my business. As an entrepreneur, this was one of the best decisions that I could have ever made. Once I let go and asked for help, the doors just kept opening for my business. I was invited to speak at a Women's Expo literally two weeks after I hired my coach! I have been asked to speak on my most passionate topic, "How to Kick Sugar Cravings," where I educate people on the detrimental physical and emotional effects that sugar has on our body. Today my business is thriving and continues to grow, and I am finally moving forward. As for my chronic pain…I don't know if I will ever come to grips with it. But, what I can tell you is that although my experience was extremely painful, the journey of learning to ask for help led me to uncover and remove roadblocks that were keeping me from my own entrepreneurial success.

When I hit my lowest point, I realized in that moment that I needed help coping with my chronic pain. Once I reached out and asked for help, I was able to power through my bad habits and addictions that were feeding my depression. Similarly, finding my passion in life and then admitting that I couldn't do it all on my own lead me to finding a coach, which was a revelation for my business. I had to learn that the roadblocks I was experiencing had nothing to do with my work, and everything to do with myself and my mentality. Asking for help is hard, but you don't have to do it on your own – I know this now. No matter if you have bad habits, addictions, depression, or you feel you are stuck in your business, reach out!

Today, my success is ME! My milestone for my success is how I have been able to overcome the roadblocks that were holding me back. I am like a tree; my health and my business are just two of my many branches. If I have bad habits and/or addictions which make me unhealthy and take me away from my goals, how am I to move forward and continue to grow? You have to do things for your own success, both personally and in business. Another branch on my tree is that I created a Health and Wellness room in my home, and I do not take my health for granted. I have "non-negotiables" that I do everyday to continue to take care of myself first, which allows me to keep moving forward. This keeps me focused on my passion of helping others create healthy habits that are sustainable, and to guide them to be the "best version of themselves." I help others find out what is stopping them, slowing them down, and keeping them from having the health and wellness that they want.

I am grateful for my journey, as my personal transformation was the impetus in starting my business. My hope for sharing this story with you is that if you are struggling with bad habits, addictions, and emotional and/or physical pain, or if you are feeling stuck as an entrepreneur, that you dig deep. I encourage and empower you to reach out, ask for help, and find a mentor, a coach, psychologist, family or friend; find someone who can help you look at your habits and figure out what is holding you back. It might not be your business that is stuck, it might be "you"!

Figure out what your passion is, find out who you are through that passion, declare what you want, and watch the doors of *your* success open! Make a choice and take a chance, so that your life can change.

About Trish Tansley

Trish is a Holistic Health & Wellness coach who is on a crusade to educate as many people as possible on sugar and the detrimental effects that it has on our bodies, both physically and emotionally. She has a passion for offering education and support in order to help you find out what is stopping you, slowing you down, or keeping you from having the health and wellness that you desire. Remember, being healthy starts on the inside.

Trish's other passion is music. She has been a vocalist for over twenty-five years and has been involved with many different music scenes, including singing the National Anthem a cappella at ball games and on National Television for a National Guard Troop of 3000 returning from the Gulf War in 1991. She is also involved in several different bands with her life partner, Scott. You hear their passion for music when they sing.

She has two beautiful grown children, Katy and Phillip, and couldn't be prouder of her grandson, Avery. Trish loves spending time and playing board games with Scott and her four step kids, Autumn, Erin, Matthew, and Talon, as well as spending time with her parents when they visit.

To start you on your health and wellness journey, Trish just has one question: "If I could wave a magic wand, and you could get the health and wellness that you want, what would that look like?"

www.holistichealthyhabits.ca
Email: HOheHA@shaw.ca
Facebook: Holistic Healthy Habits
Instagram: luvHOheHA
LinkedIn: trish-tansley-holistic health coach

9

DESIGN AND LIFE

by Michelle Bernier

"Good design is capturing the spirit of the client in the soul of the space."
Michelle Bernier

Design and Life

by Michelle Bernier

Design and life are very similar. You appreciate beauty and function, you want to feel safe and loved and you want your space to be enjoyable and comfortable for you and your family for years to come. Be the designer of your life and plan out the perfect scenario that will make you happy.

I grew up in a large family with two brothers and seven sisters, a place where you can easily get lost in the crowd and lose your identity. You become one of the "clan" instead of being acknowledged as an individual. I was a middle child – fifth from the bottom and sixth from the top – and it meant that I was often not old enough to do certain things but too old for others. Forging a trail towards more independence helped me form my entrepreneurial skills throughout my childhood. I didn't realize the significance at the time, but ideas always came to me in the form of plans or a direction to go. I didn't know how to successfully implement these notions, but my clarity was in the big picture rather than the small details.

My role model for being passionate about what you do was my mom. She started dancing when she was young, and she danced professionally until she met my dad. Even after marrying him and having ten children, she always longed to go back to dancing. She started taking ballroom classes with my father for fun, but she soon discovered her love of dance again and in her forties she started competing. She travelled for competitions and won trophies and medals. When my youngest sister was four, my mom decided to start her own school, so she could teach her girls how to dance. She had no experience in opening or running a business, but she forged ahead and started the Dupre School of Dance which stayed open for over thirty years. We were known as the Dupre Sisters, which was just another way of saying we fought a lot. When you and your seven sisters are taking dance classes taught by your mom, it becomes a war zone. Someone was always mad or walking out or fighting with someone else, and god forbid if someone got the step quicker or grew faster and got moved up the line – especially if they were younger. Through all the turmoil and the in-fighting, my mother continued to teach us. However, she taught us more than dance; she taught us to persevere and to work with your passion and strengths. She always said, "anyone can learn to dance," and spent thirty years proving that statement. She passed away in 2000 from breast cancer, but even at the end she still really wanted to dance. Her passion shone brightly all her life; she was remarkable in that way.

Finding My Passion

I have had several businesses, including a toy store and an accounting firm, but while I enjoyed owning a business I never felt completely satisfied. I wasn't passionate about what I was doing. I would dive head first into my newest venture, but then I would lose focus. Been there, done that!

I always loved to design and decorate, and I worked hard to create beauty in my home. I could see if something needed to be moved or added or expanded or removed to create something more beautiful, more functional, or more well-designed. I had a strange love for lighting and chairs, and I was always very good at colour matching – even if I didn't always understand why it all worked together. I decided to explore this side of myself, so I signed up for a night school course in interior design to improve my knowledge. Much to my amazement, this decision ended up changing my entire career and focus. I ended up going through the entire interior design program at night while working all day in my business. It was a crazy time! I worked hard, taking as many courses as I could each semester so I could finish early. I was focused and wanted to be done. However, once I finished I thought…what now? With no experience and no customers, I continued working on my other business while I built up my clientele.

Shortly after I finished school, two things happened that changed my direction. One day I was standing on a chair to put up decorations for my daughters 9th birthday. When I tried to reach the other wall, I tipped the chair and fell. I hit the floor with my elbow and shattered my arm right at the elbow joint. I had to have surgery, I couldn't work effectively, and I had to significantly downsize my accounting business and move my office back into my home. This felt like moving backwards instead of forward, but in retrospect it allowed me to focus on design instead of on accounting. While I recovered, my time was spent reflecting on what I wanted to do now and how to achieve it.

About six months after my injury, the next big change happened: I was suddenly offered an opportunity to start a design business with two more experienced partners. I excitedly jumped in, but it became quickly apparent that the other partners didn't understand how much work is required to start a new business. They bailed in fast succession, and I was left alone with a three-year lease, a brand-new business that hadn't made any money, and all the responsibility. I had invested a great deal of money into the business so I needed to make this work. However, I was a new designer with no experience and I was scared that I would fail miserably. I wasn't afraid to have ideas, but making them work effectively was challenging. I was getting so bogged down in the details that at times I was drowning. I wanted to create something new, but I didn't know if I was good enough to do it. I doubted myself, my talent, my business model and everything that I had just created. I had to take a leap of faith; it was challenging and hard, but in the end there wasn't any other option. Making this business work became my vision.

Did I make mistakes? Of course! I always felt like I was on the brink of failure or disaster, but I just wouldn't give up no matter what. Running a business can be devastating, but how you deal with the obstacles is key. Okay, I admit that sometimes I cried and obsessed over the bad things that happened – things like broken leases, losing clients, supplier issues or just the stress of day-to-day business – but eventually, I realized that focusing on the bad things really wasn't worth my time and was just preventing me from moving forward. Learning to get back up and to wish someone well, but away, was how my life changed for the better. Sometimes when something didn't work out as planned, the new situation was even better than I was aiming for in the first place; you never know what is behind door number two unless you close door number one.

Be a visionary and don't get bogged down in the details. How do you sculpt Venus De Milo? Chisel away everything that isn't Venus De Milo. In my business, I see the finished design in my head and work towards that. I listen to my client, pull their ideas out of their head, and design for their unique personality to create their space. I infuse their soul into the design by chiseling away everything that isn't them. Ta dah! There is the magic!

The Effects of Colour

Everyone deserves a space that is home to them, which is why I started my charity, Design With Hope. I feel that battered women and children deserve to have a space that is beautiful, safe, and special. A little paint may seem small in comparison to their problems, but coming home to a place that you love and colours that inspire you can brighten your mood and make you feel at peace. Maybe, for these women, seeing their favorite colour splashed on the walls will spark a seed of hopefulness and make their life a tiny bit brighter every day. That is a lot of bang for your buck out of a simple can of paint!

I love the look on the children's faces when they pick their colour out. They will ask, "I can pick ANY colour? Anything at all?" It's the proverbial kid in a candy store. Children know immediately what they love and what they want. They react to colour very positively and with great passion. They LOVE red or pink or blue or green. They instinctively know what colours makes them feel good, and they want it in huge quantities.

This reaction is why I have one rule for kid's rooms: the child picks the colour of their bedroom. It's their space, and it should reflect them at that moment in time. One of my favorite stories is from a client who was painting their ten-year-old daughter's room. She selected a beautiful shade of deep purple that she absolutely adored. Once her dad started painting, though, he phoned me and said, "This is too bright, it's too purple, this will not be good at all. It must be changed." I replied, "Just continue painting. You can always close the door if you don't want to see the purple, but it's her space and it makes her feel good. Trust me on this."

He begrudgingly finished painting the room, and his daughter was ecstatic. She showed the colour off to all her friends, she hung out in her room more often, and she spent more time doing homework there. As for the dad, it turned out to be his favourite room in the house. He would often go into the room and lay on the bed so he could enjoy the colour. He felt happy in that space. In the end, he felt what his daughter felt when she picked the colour. That was a powerful lesson to me on the effects of colour, and on how people react to it.

We all have our favorite colours. However, certain colours can affect your mental and physical state, running a whole gamut of emotions. Colour psychology has been around for a long time, and has shown that specific colour can make you feel a certain way. Pink has a calming effect while red can energize you. Yellow can help you focus while blue and green can improve your mood. Which ones will work for you in your home, your office or your newborn baby's room?

Respect Your Clients

Clients always need understand that you respect their home. It is their most personal and most sacred space. The first and most important rule all designers should follow is that *it's not your home.* You can design a gorgeous modern space, but if your client loves traditional styles and wood finishes then they'll never enjoy it. It doesn't matter what your personal preferences are, your job is to design their space to suit their lifestyle and their personality.

A client's treasures should also be respected. They can and should be used in their space, although they may need an update to really bring them to life. Your husband's university chair, with the springs falling out and the ratty fabric, may remind him of a simpler time in life and bring him joy. By reupholstering it, you can make it work in your new space. The photo of Granny from the 1890's can be reframed and set with other black and white photos for a stunning wall display. Balance, colour and textures are what bring a room together and make it special and unique.

The best way to make a client happy is to listen, listen, listen! Something small can be the key to the design, such as the fact that they collect seashells because it reminds them of the beach. You just listen to what the client is saying – or, in some cases, not saying. Clients may feel they have to like a certain style, even though deep down they prefer something else. As a designer you can always make something look great, but the challenge is if you can make someone feel great in their space! That is the fine line between designing and being a designer.

The greatest compliment I can get is for someone to say, "It's exactly what I want!" They get to see the design in their head become a reality, and sometimes they are completely shocked by how much they love it; sometimes they didn't know it's what they wanted until they saw the final product. Good design has its own personality.

Working directly with clients does come with challenges, though. They can test your patience, your wisdom and make you wonder why you went into business. They may not understand the design or the process it takes to get there, or they simply want to second guess your recommendations. There are many different client types and personalities, just like in life. For example, one client insisted on changing the design over and over, because they thought maybe something better was out there. It was exhausting, but it helped me learn to be patient but firm.

I also had to learn that you can't make everyone happy. I once had a client whom I was trying so hard to please. I had gone out of my way to give her everything she asked for and make it more affordable for her, delivered to her free of charge, and gave her more ideas for other areas in her home. I was trying so hard to keep her that I was giving myself away. It didn't make her appreciate me more, and I wasn't happy with giving my creativity and talents away to someone who didn't see my vision or value my worth as a designer. She was not the right fit for me or my business.

Sometimes in life, we are not the right fit at that time, in that space, at that moment. If you keep trying to put the round peg in the square hole, it's never going to fit properly. Learn to accept these moments when they arrive, because it means that something better was destined to be there.

Working With the Trades

The misconception that many people have is that trades are difficult and hard to manage effectively, and that can certainly be true for a homeowner with one project to complete. However, as a repeat customer with many projects throughout the year I have more influence with them. I have three rules for the trades I hire:

1. Be polite to clients and call me first if there is an issue. I like to give the client the solution instead of the problem.
2. Clean up after yourself; don't leave your mess for another trade to clean up. Be respectful of the client's home.
3. Take pride in your workmanship and always give the best quality job to the client, even if it takes longer.

These rules don't just apply to the trades though! They are mantras that everyone should follow: be polite, clean up after yourself, and take pride in yourself!

Sometimes I find working with people in the trades challenging because we think very differently. They look at the job and try to complete it in the least number of steps required, while as a designer I look at the job and try to complete it in a unique and interesting way. I don't always care if the details take longer, so long as the final result is what I planned.

That being said, people in the trades also want to have their work shine and be appreciated. Clients don't always appreciate the effort that the trades make in their projects, but I sure do. When we work as an effective team, the result is amazing and the client is happy and satisfied. I respect advice they give me, and in turn they respect that a good design will make their work look better. These are the trades I align with and that I want for my client's projects, because design cannot happen without execution. When I work with people I respect and who respect me, the client gets the best job, for the best price, with the best quality. Good trades are vital to this industry, and my trades are an asset to my business and extremely valuable.

If you hire a trade, make sure you have a clear plan, a good vision and can discuss the plan in a reasonable way. Be open to suggestions and see the big picture. When there is mutual respect, the sky is the limit!

Design Your Life

Be the designer of your own business, create from beauty and purpose, and don't let anyone tell you it cannot be done. Life and business are your creation, so make them the best that they can be! Bring in colour and textures that uniquely reflect you and your soul. Work within your limits, then go past those limits and try new ideas, even if you aren't sure if it's the right time or if everyone is telling you not to. Commit to your business idea, but be coachable. Listen, learn, and discover something that didn't exist before you created it. Take pride in your business that you created from nothing, and that is now flourishing. Your business is individual and unique, just like you.

Imagine someone giving you a standing ovation every day, even if you feel like you have failed. Remember, you got up and continued to go forward and that is worthy of applause! Every day isn't going to be a winning design, but every day you can take another step closer to your goal. Inspire yourself in the beauty of the creation, even if you don't have the entire design finished. Don't forget to laugh and be okay with some mistakes along the way. By doing so, you learn a great lesson in patience, acceptance, and moving forward.

Design your life to reflect your dream and vision. It should fit your style and your personality, and it should celebrate you. You are the designer and creator of your life, so make it the best one possible!

About Michelle Bernier

Michelle Bernier has loved interior design since she was a child, and is in her natural element when she is designing and creating amazing spaces for her clients. She has been in the renovation and design business for over ten years and has proven that she can deliver a beautiful finished project. Her clients love her innovative ideas and fresh approach to decorating and design.

Michelle's constant pursuit for excellence, design, and innovation, coupled with her affinity for using Canadian products, make her a well-sought-after designer. Michelle also has strong personal values and is loyal to her clients, friends, suppliers and to the underprivileged in her community. She is passionate that design should be beautiful, functional, and unique to you.

Her husband, Rey, and her two beautiful children, James and Anaiyah, have enhanced her creativity for making spaces beautiful throughout the years.

Her company, Michelle Dupré Design & Company, is a one-stop design shop for all of your project needs, from cabinetry to tiles, paint, wallpaper, flooring, fabrics and more. She has taught design to many students and plans to create more design classes as part of her business model.

www.MichelleDupreDesign.com
Email: michelle@michelledupredesign.com
Facebook: designwithconfidence

10

FROM SHADOWS TO SPARKLES

by Stephanie "Sparkles" Lehr

"Well I'm just like Patsy, I got my sparkle back again"
Nice and Slow
Boy George

From Shadows to Sparkles

by Stephanie "Sparkles" Lehr

November 6th, 2012. This date is a defining moment in my life, one that sent me down a path from grief to triumph, but my story actually starts way before then. I wish to take you on my journey from being a shy shadow of a little curly-haired, red-headed girl to becoming the empowered, sparkling woman and entrepreneur that I am today.

I was born in Ottawa, Canada, in 1970 to a very loving family comprised of my parents, my two brothers, and my twin sister. When I look back, I feel that I had an "abnormally normal" childhood; my upbringing was a traditional, conservative one typical of the 70's, with roles and division of labour defined by gender.

My identical twin sister and I did everything together. We dressed alike, played with the same toys, and read the same books. We were typically referred to as "the girls" or "the twins." However, when I was eleven years old, I started to resent being a twin, a package deal, "me and my shadow." I desperately wanted to be *me*, but I didn't really know who that was. My identity was so intertwined with my sister that it was hard to step out from my comfortable spot in her shadow.

Throughout my pre-teen and teen years, I also began to grapple with gender inequality. I hated having to do certain household chores just because I was female, and I was dismayed when I realized there was violence against women just because they were women. This knowledge made me feel such unrest in my heart, and it set the stage for my interest in gender equality and female empowerment. It also kick-started my mission to serve various woman-centred organizations.

In 1989 I graduated from Grade Thirteen, and I felt like the upcoming prom was my chance to be different. I picked a beautiful light blue satin dress that I thought would stand out from the crowd. However, I soon discovered that one of my classmates, who had actually sold me my dress, was wearing the exact same one, just in a different colour. I was absolutely mortified! I wanted to feel unique and special, and now that had been taken away from me. I didn't know it at the time, but this event would prove to be a defining moment that guided my future business.

In the next twenty years I graduated from university, got married, and found a full-time job in the private sector. However, I often felt that I was just going through the motions of life. I wanted to make a difference in the work that I was doing, but it always seemed like there was something lacking or that there was something else that I was meant to do... something more.

By 2011, I was aching to try something new. I've always marvelled at and respected people who could create something like architecture, poetry, art, and crafts, but I never thought that

I was particularly creative. Then one day I picked up a book on jewellery-making and thought, *I can do this*. I was so excited! It felt like I had found the missing piece in my life. I created jewellery for my entire family as a surprise for Christmas, and I was told I should keep making more and actually sell some pieces.

Encouraged by my family, I started to hone my craft by taking a jewellery class and I researched how to start a small business. On July 18th, 2012, I opened an online shop called Sparkle Designs By Stephanie. I applied for a provincial business license and started to create jewellery pieces in my spare time as I was still working full-time in the private sector. It was a challenge to do both as my day job was demanding and mentally draining on the best of days, but I had found my passion and others seemed to like my work and continued to encourage me. This gave me the motivation to keep pushing forward.

I thought a lot about my branding, business name, messaging, and why I created my business. It was important to me that it wasn't just about the jewellery or external sparkle; I wanted to ensure that the internal sparkle was also honoured, which guided me to create the tagline "Wear...Feel...Share." Additionally, every piece that I create is a one-of-a-kind, one-off piece to celebrate the individual who wears it. Creating unique pieces ties directly back to my prom dress experience. I've always felt that each person is special, and so their jewellery should be as well. With every purchase, I include a card with the following message: "Each SDS piece is uniquely created with an element of sparkle with the intention to inspire your inner sparkle to positively affect others in the world."

Stepping out and creating jewellery for the public did have its challenges. I worried about whether my work was good enough, whether I would be criticized, whether people would like them, whether they would fall apart, the list goes on. Quite frankly, due to the materials I originally used, some pieces were not exceptional. However, I was given feedback by my customers that allowed me to better understand the importance of quality over quantity, customer service, and integrity. It's so important to have these learnings and to humbly grow and persevere.

In 2012, I had big dreams for my online jewellery business. I was making plans to gradually switch to working part-time in my day job and then eventually quit entirely so I could become full-time in my jewellery business. I felt like I was fulfilling my purpose in the world, spreading my sparkle and encouraging others to share their own.

November 6th, 2012, that defining day in my life, started like any other Tuesday. I was watching the morning news on TV when my husband informed me that he no longer wished to be married. He said that he hoped we could remain amicable, that I would be alright as I had a lot of things going for me, and that I would thank him in five years. I had no clue that he was feeling this way! I felt like a failure, and I was ashamed that after twenty years of marriage I would now be a divorce statistic. He moved out a month later, and once he was gone I hid from the world out of embarrassment.

It was hard to tell my family what had happened as divorce was frowned upon. I only told my immediate relatives and a few close friends about the situation; I was too ashamed to tell anyone else and I could barely speak without crying. I rarely left the house. I wouldn't answer the phone or the door for fear of having to explain what was going on, and I was always on edge and worried that someone would find out. Deep down, I also secretly thought that we would still work this out somehow, and if I didn't tell too many people that we were separating then there would be less people to update when we got back together.

In 2013, I lost my passion and I stopped making jewellery altogether. I would walk aimlessly throughout my so-called dream home, alone and sad that my dreams were snuffed out by a person who had committed to loving me. I would walk by the Sparkle Studio, shut the door, and keep going. I deactivated my online store. I didn't feel loved, creative, worthy, or confident; my Sparkle was gone. I had frequent episodes of uncontrollable sobbing and self-judgment. There was even a time when I thought that suicide may be easier than going through a divorce and living with so much pain. I have my family to thank for their unconditional love and encouragement, which helped me get back on the right track. Eventually, I sought out a counsellor through my Employee Assistance Program and started going to church for extra support.

During this time, I discovered Twitter and realized that my childhood hero, Boy George, had an account. I had first discovered him when I was twelve, along with the musical group Culture Club. I was immediately attracted to him because he was such a unique individual, with outspoken messages of "different is good" and "just be yourself." He had a profound impact on me when I was young as I desperately wanted to be different too. Seeing his name inspired me to create my own account, although I had no picture and only a partial name. I still didn't want to be found by people who might ask me about my marital status.

Boy George and I followed one another, and my life changed for the better. I was captivated by his art, music, photography, vegetarian cooking, DJing, and spirituality; he was a free individual spirit. He was living his creative life out loud after overcoming some low points of his own. I began to feel inspired again, and I decided to make some choices for myself, such as becoming a vegetarian and embracing being different. I was coming out of the shadows.

In 2014, I went to Toronto to see my first Boy George concert. I had brought with me a jewellery piece that I designed specifically for him, and I had hoped to give it to him as a thank you gift for inspiring me. The necklace did make its way to George and, to my utmost surprise, he wore it during his performances for the rest of the tour. Not wanting attention and living below the radar, I chose not to share this on Twitter and instead kept silent. I was comfortable with being comfortable.

In May 2014, I sold my home and moved to the Fraser Valley area in British Columbia, Canada so I could be close to my family. I bought a house and continued work full-time in the private sector. Later that year, I begrudgingly joined Facebook so I could vote for Boy George in a DJ poll. Suddenly, I received friend requests from all sorts of people. I was quite overwhelmed as I didn't know anything about Facebook and just wanted to remain hidden. Again, I didn't want to explain why I moved, or why my husband didn't come with me. I reluctantly friended others and used a caricature of myself for my profile.

On December 12th, 2014, I met a lovely man with two children and discovered love, a deep love that I had not realized existed. He is an emotional, loving, caring, thoughtful, supportive, funny, and high-energy man. I had found my life partner.

My partner was always encouraging me to get out of my comfort zone, but I resisted. I was insistent that he not post photos of me on social media as I didn't want any attention or people looking at me. Eventually, after much persuasion, I trusted him enough to let him put some photos of me online.

To my surprise, no one was unkind; in fact, they were just the opposite. I started to get comfortable with being *uncomfortable*, I gained more confidence, and I branched out and began trying new things.

In August 2015, my partner and his son moved in with me, and automatically my house became a home. Later that year, I also decided it was time to start my online part-time jewellery business again. I created a Facebook business page, Sparkle Designs By Stephanie, and began designing one-of-a-kind pieces and getting positive feedback and sales. I got my Sparkle back again!

During this time, I finally had the courage to pursue the necessary paperwork for my divorce as I wanted to close that chapter of my life. Even though I had moved past the embarrassment and shame I had felt, I was still quite guarded with others.

In mid-2017, I felt like I was missing out on connections with other business women. I had been working out of a home office for my day job since 2010, and I was running an online jewellery business where I didn't meet anyone face-to-face. Additionally, I had just moved to a new province without knowing anyone outside of my family. It was time to let people know that I existed. It was time to come out of the shadows.

In July that same year, I discovered a networking group and I went to their signature patio party event with fancy dresses and fascinators. I didn't know anyone, and truth be told I didn't even know what a fascinator was! Regardless, I went and met some friendly, inspiring ladies. This event led me to other relationships, sponsorships, and friendships, both in person and online. Making that decision to connect was one of the best things I have ever done! Through connection, I have had the chance to sponsor community events and causes that are close to my heart, including those serving in mental health, anti-bullying, girl and women empowerment, LGBTQ2+, and animal rights. I can't tell you the joy and gratitude I feel in making a difference in the lives of others.

While I am becoming more visible in the community, people are getting to know, like, and trust me. They learn what I stand for and what my business and brand are all about. It's important to me that people know that community, service, quality, excellence, kindness, gratitude, and fun are the core values at the heart of what I do. When I look for a project, it has to be in alignment with these core values; otherwise, I make the decision to pass.

I have taken a lot of small steps to come out of the shadows and Sparkle in 2017. I took my first selfie with no make-up, and I recorded my first video and posted it on social media. I took over hosting duties with a women's networking group and posted content two to three times per week for a month. I've participated in video-based networking meetings, and my goals are to become more comfortable with live video and to try other social media platforms. All of these steps are milestones for me and have really helped my confidence in my business. By sharing them with others, I believe it will help others feel that they can do it too.

As I was meeting new people, building relationships, collaborating on projects, and fostering friendships, it came to me: Sparkle Designs By Stephanie is much more than jewellery. It is a brand under which I encourage, inspire, and motivate women to step up, step out, and Sparkle. Inspired, I decided it was time to leverage my brand and move the needle forward. At the time of writing this chapter, I have initiated my new online series, "Sparkle Spirit Spotlight," with the intention of highlighting entrepreneurs in a written series with my "Motiv8

Q&A." This will be marketed on social media with the goal of inspiring others to share their Sparkle.

My decision to step out of the shadows is leading me to new and meaningful collaborations with community sponsorships, public relations, media, retail boutiques, and technology innovation for my business. I am taking steps toward my dream of working full-time in my passion. I am grateful for my upbringing, my family, and all of my experiences that have led me to this moment of sharing my story. I have to say thank you, and I'm so excited for the future!

On November 6th, 2017, I posted a message on social media to honour the journey I have made from grief to determined independence:

"Thank you...what a difference 5 years can make:

Flash flood, spring of tears
Deep channel; capsizing all fears.
Single stream running...
-by Miss Stephanie Sparkles"

My purpose for sharing my story and the challenges I've faced is to encourage, inspire, and motivate you. Perhaps you are someone experiencing a personal setback, like a divorce, or perhaps you are looking to make a change in your career. Maybe you are someone with an entrepreneurial Sparkle Spirit with a passion to start a business, and you aren't really sure if you can. You feel you lack confidence, support, and resources. You've been feeling this way for a while and haven't taken any action because it's easier not to. You are comfortably living in your own shadow.

I want to leave you with this quote from Marianne Williamson. When I heard this quote for the first time on The Oprah Winfrey

Show, I sat up in my chair and listened, cried, and then rewound it a few more times so I could take it in.

"Our deepest fear is not that we are inadequate. Our deepest fear is that we are powerful beyond measure. It is our light, not our darkness, that most frightens us. We ask ourselves, 'Who am I to be brilliant, gorgeous, talented, fabulous?' Actually, who are you not to be? You are a child of God. Your playing small does not serve the world. There is nothing enlightened about shrinking so that other people won't feel insecure around you. We are all meant to shine, as children do. We were born to make manifest the glory of God that is within us. It's not just in some of us; it's in everyone. And as we let our own light shine, we unconsciously give other people permission to do the same. As we are liberated from our own fear, our presence automatically liberates others." (Marianne Williamson, "A Return to Love")

So I say to you, dear reader: shine, don't shrink! Consider changing not just your mind, but your mindset. Set some goals, do some research, read all you can, join some networking groups, ask questions, ask for help, make mistakes, take courses in your area of interest, and find support. Look for a mentor who can guide you; there are some really awesome, kickass women out there who are willing to help! Dream, then dream bigger. You need to know that you matter. You are valued. You are valuable. The world needs your unique gifts and talents; only *you* can do *you*!

Just put yourself out there, and focus on progress over perfection; otherwise, the world may never get to see your gifts and talents. And above all, I encourage you to "step up, step out, and Sparkle...and while you're at it, leave a trail."

About Stephanie "Sparkles" Lehr

Stephanie is the Jewellery Designer/ Owner and Sparkle Strategist of Sparkle Designs By Stephanie, a company created to serve you and your Sparkle, inside and out. She helps you Sparkle by offering you meaningful, memorable, one-of-a-kind, one-off jewellery pieces to help you stand out from the rest, or for you to give to your client as a way to express your gratitude for their business and loyalty.

Since 2012, she has been incorporating stunning gemstones, sterling silver, and Swarovski pearls and crystals into her creations, which are inspired by her clients, nature, art, poetry, and music. Her pieces have made their way to adorn influencers and even some celebrities.

Coming soon, Stephanie will also be offering a brand new Sparkle Spirit Suite to serve your inner Sparkle! The Suite will include but is not limited to a motivational entrepreneurial Sparkle Spirit Spotlight series, Sparkle Rituals, and Sparkle merchandise.

Stephanie also believes in helping communities Sparkle by collaborating on impactful events and causes closest to her heart, including those serving in mental health, anti-bullying, girl and women empowerment, LGBTQ2+, and animal rights.

Originally from Ottawa, Canada, Stephanie has been living in the picturesque Fraser Valley Lower Mainland area in British Columbia, Canada for the past few years with her loving partner, Norm. She is "Steph-Mom" to two amazing teens: fear-loving stepson, Jake, and fun-loving stepdaughter, Macy.

www.SparkleDesignsByStephanie.com
Facebook: Stephanie Sparkles or Sparkle Designs By Stephanie
Instagram: @StephanieSparkles88
Email: SparkleDesignsByStephanie@gmail.com

11

RE-PLANTING SEEDS

by Sandra Fikus

"Everything happens for a reason and as it should."
Sandra Fikus

Re-planting Seeds

by Sandra Fikus

As I was lying on the couch after surviving another day of chemo, I saw a program called the Spa of Embarrassing Illnesses. The program was about six people who were taken away to a spa-like resort where they explored and received both modern and traditional modes of healing. It highlighted how along our journey through life, things happen – whether we are aware of them or not – that not only influence our lives but our health too. These experiences, no matter how insignificant, can and do have an effect on our emotional and physical health. While cancer was not one of the illnesses represented, I felt like they were speaking directly to me.

After seeing this show, I decided that I wanted to create a facility where both medical and alternative practitioners were brought together; a place where someone can get all the care they need under one roof. I wasn't working and had the means to seek out different therapies that helped me get through chemotherapy, but I had to go searching for it on my own. One specialist I found that opened this path was my Dr. Mary; she is a Chinese Medicine Doctor, and thirty minutes with her, along with six needles, completely removed the need to take pills to ease the side effects of the chemo. It was meeting her that sent me in search of anything I could find to go forward and discover other alternative treatments which would help me heal.

After I recovered from chemo, radiation, and later a mastectomy and reconstruction, one of my friends – who knew I was interested in getting back into business – mentioned that the owner of a medical centre was looking for another partner. My kids had been bugging me to get a job, but after being my own boss in a company I helped build with my spouse, I could not go back to being an employee. I also didn't need to be employed, so I only wanted to return to work if it was for something meaningful. So, I said I would be willing to meet with her to find out more.

We met one night over drinks; I had seen her before when I was a client of the clinic but did not formally know her. We had a good meeting, and she was very enthusiastic and positive. I realized later that she was just desperate. She was going through her own personal hell because, as I later found out, she was just days away from locking the doors. We met a few more times and agreed that, pending the financial statements, I would become a 20% partner; I was not willing to fully jump in as there were many red flags which should have sent me running. I just had a feeling.

I started July 3, 2013. When I walked in I not only saw the potential, I also saw the problems. The clinic was paying an expensive monthly lease payment for the equipment, which I discovered should have only been half of what it was. The owner I had met with was collecting a large salary that made up half of the total payroll, and the other partner, who was a doctor, was squatting for free. He left shortly after. I could write a whole book on the drama that happened for the next two months; the deceit, dishonesty, fraud, and theft which I will be so bold as to say. I knew it was critical to get the last partner out. It all came to a boiling point when a guy showed up and started taking pictures, which she said was for insurance. It took her several days to tell me it was a bailiff, and if we didn't come up with $20K by Monday they would chain the doors. I had her sign over 51% of the company to me, because I was dishing out of all the money and she had nothing. She was reluctant, but eventually gave in. I learned later that while this was going on she was trying to sell my shares to someone else, saying I was only a small partner.

All of this happened within three months of me starting.

The morning of our meeting with the lawyers to finalize the change in shares, we both came to work. At the end of the day we left out of separate doors at the same time, and one of my managers said she knew that only one of us were coming back. I knew, too; I had to get her out.

The meeting took maybe ten minutes, and she looked like a deer caught in headlights. When it was over the lawyers and I congratulated each other as we had just accomplished the shortest take over in history, although I knew there was more work to come. What did I just take on?

I could write a book, not just a chapter, on the things that happened next and the lessons I learned, both about myself and about business. Many of my challenges were buried at the very heart of me, from seeds that were planted a long time ago. Trying to prove my worth is a struggle I've fought with my whole life.

As a woman entrepreneur, this is the advice I would give.

1. Be specific in your intentions

I am a true believer in the Law of Attraction. There is a quote that says, "Everything is energy and that's all there is to it. Match the frequency of the reality you want and you cannot help but get that reality. It can be no other way. It is not philosophy. This is physics." I have found this to be true my whole life. When you really look back, you can see it; however, if you are not specific, what you get back may look a different than what you had hoped. I got exactly what I wanted when I set my intentions out that day, lying on the couch recovering from chemo. I just should have thrown in that the business should not be moments away from sinking to the bottom of ocean! But then, would I have got what I wanted? The extra money I had to invest is relevant. I could have never started this clinic from scratch on my own; I came from a totally different industry, so I simply didn't have the contacts. That's the cost of doing business, and you have to be prepared.

We get exactly what we put out to the universe, even if it's what you don't want; The Laws of Attraction don't distinguish the good from the bad. So, if you spend all day focusing on the negative aspects of your life, then that's what you'll get more of! This doesn't mean we have to be happy every minute; just find moments to put what you want out there more often. We get exactly what we align our thoughts and vibration to.

2. Be patient

Good things come to those who wait. This is true, and it can be extremely frustrating at times. You see the vision, but things are not yet in place. I remember when my spouse and I started our first company, we only had it for a year before he started getting frustrated that we weren't profitable yet. He was willing to sell the entire company to one of the other partners for what he put into it. I told him that you have to be willing to put in four to five years before you will start to see profits, so we had to hang in there. This turned out to be correct; the only problem is that our relationship didn't last that long.

Now here I am, in the fourth year of my business, constantly reminding myself that we are exactly on track. I cannot go to work every day and get excited if I am thinking we are failing. We are not losing money, we know exactly where it is spent. Our revenue just has not built up enough to exceed our expenses. That why you have to be patient, and you have to know that being in business means taking chances. There is a saying I read years ago: in order to get to the fruit on the tree, you have to go out on a limb. And you must be prepared to be the last one paid!

3. Be passionate

You have to be passionate and believe in what you're doing. My previous company was not a sexy, innovative medical facility; it was a janitorial company. Our passion was simply that we all had the drive to make it work, and that is what we did. It was risky for my partner and I, especially after we had our kids, as we had a lot riding on the company. But we were passionate about it, and when I left it was heartbreaking for me.

Not everyone is cut out to own their own business; it sounds romantic, but being the boss is hard. If you're not prepared to make sacrifices and put your employees before yourself, then don't do it.

If you can't take the risk of quitting your day job, then doing your business on the side is always an option. Put yourself into the mindset of allowing, though. Imagine and feel what it's like to be successful. Just because you have not achieved it yet, doesn't mean you cannot feel it. Enjoy the process of manifestation.

4. Be good to yourself

When life gets busy, stressful, and difficult, self-care is one of the most important practices to keep up. However, it tends to be the one thing that we neglect when going through these challenging times. I learned about self-care in my twenties when I was on my spiritual path. It's not just about diet and exercise; it's also about taking care of your mind and heart. The best book out there on this topic is "The Power of Positive Thinking" by Reverend Norman Vincent Peal, which I read at least every couple of years.

Before I bought the business, I was taking care of myself; I meditated, exercised, and ate well, but I also enjoyed dating and going out on the town. It was a good life. However, in business, things were moving slow and my stress hit a peak in 2015. I had spent hundreds of thousands of dollars of my savings. Even though things were moving forward, I still could not see this light at the end of tunnel and was seriously looking at whether bankruptcy was my best option. I was also privately dealing with my own embarrassment of getting myself into this situation. I have an MBA so I should have known better than to invest in a business that I wasn't fully confident in, but I wanted it. When people would ask me how it was going, I would just say "fine." I would also say I was "fine" on chemo. Sometimes fine means you hit bottom.

Around this time, I started to notice seeds of self-doubt that were planted when I was younger. My dad had told me that I would never make it on my own; I would either have to win it or marry into it. That's what his upbringing had taught him. The challenges with my business had me wondering if maybe, possibly, he was right.

I stopped going out and instead began coming home and rewarding myself for surviving another hard day with a glass of wine. Eventually this turned into a bottle of wine or more and a half pack of smokes. Then I was also dealing with the guilt of being hungover, tired, and ashamed of being a cancer survivor and wellness centre owner who went home and smoked and drank too much. For the next year I sunk into some very dark places, and if it wasn't for my kids and some very special friends I would have just disappeared.

When you go to these hard places, keeping up your self-care practices is extremely important. During this time, a friend introduced me to Theta meditation. Once I began this practice the constant knot in my stomach started to loosen. Eventually, I finally snapped out of it and got my life in order. This doesn't mean I don't slip up and have some wine or light up the occasional cigarette – I won't put that pressure on myself – but I see now, more than at any other point in my life, that I can't take care of others without taking care of myself. If I didn't, I wouldn't be writing this now.

5. Surround yourself with like-minded people

When I first started struggling with the difficulties I faced in my new business, I felt that I couldn't let people in because I thought it took away from my drive of "doing it on my own." I was also too ashamed to admit how low I was feeling. Eventually I gave in and reached out, and it was the best thing

I've done. My business is better for it.

You can't go out there and accomplish everything that you desire if you surround yourself with people that will bring you down. It just doesn't work. You need support, and asking for help doesn't take anything away from your accomplishments. When I started, there were people around me who did not have my best interests at heart, and it was a disaster. I always believed that if I was a good person, then everyone around me would be good back. However, you can't control the intentions of others. In the end I have had to let some people go, not just professionally but personally.

I now have learned who are my real friends are, and I have a lot of people in my life who I can rely on and who I can accept help from. It seems that as soon I changed and made an effort to reach out to those who I can trust, even more great people have come into my life. I've also realized the benefit of connecting with other people who know more about different aspects of business than I do.

6. Be grateful for today

What can I say about gratitude? It is so wonderful to wake up every morning and hold gratitude in your heart. Lately, I have learned the practice of having gratitude for the things I desire that have not yet manifested. We often put conditions on our life: I will be happy when this happens, when I have the perfect partner, when I have this amount of money. What we are doing is putting a condition on our happiness, and if the situation doesn't turn out exactly right then we are not happy. In order to manifest what we want into our lives, we need to feel the happiness and gratitude as if they were already here.

I have gone to some dark places where I struggled to get

out of bed, had no motivation, and wanted to disappear. I felt sorry for myself because I needed help, and I felt guilty for engaging in unhealthy behaviours in order to escape.

As a women, I have also discovered my insecurities were deeper after having cancer. Losing my breast was more dramatic than I thought, and I am reminded about it everyday when I look in the mirror. Some women say that it's only a breast, not as bad as losing an arm or a leg, but it is still a part of you. They nourished my kids and made me feel whole as a women; I would be lying if I said that it doesn't affect me everyday. I don't want my daughter to go through life with fear because of what happened to me. I don't want her to get scared into cutting off her breasts because she *might* get cancer.

Today, though, I'm seeing things differently. I am grateful for all of my experiences, not just the good but the bad as well. I am even grateful for all the bad people I've had in my life over the last four years; I know I they were in my life for a reason, and it was to make me stronger. I've learned that even though I want to treat people right, I can't let anyone walk all over me. I watch the news every day and see this is happening all over the world. Women are standing up for their worth, and it's about time!

I wake up every morning and try to follow practices that help put me in this positive mental state, and I can honestly say it has made a world of difference. Success is an ongoing process; it's never done, as business and life are constantly evolving. There is a saying that goes, "if you're green you're growing, when you're ripe you rot." I don't want to rot; it's perfectly okay to want more.

Would I do it again?

If I could do it all over again, would I? My answer might change from day to day, but when I think of all that has happened in the past ten years since my diagnosis, I cannot imagine being without the people who are in my life now. I also look back at the past ten years not just as a business experience, but as a personal one too. It turns out my biggest obstacle was my belief that I was just a girl, not capable and not worthy. While I still have to work on releasing this belief, I have made incredible progress. I am learning to accept my worth, and I no longer feel like I have to prove it to anyone. I know the purpose of my diagnosis was to teach me that I could do anything. I believe that the lump gave me the strength to make a difference rather than simply taking the easy route and accepting things the way they are.

Much of this has happened because I had cancer. I don't feel like a victim because of it, and I am not scared of it anymore. I have lost many friends to this disease, and when I get low I think of them and how they would give anything to be here. Maybe along the path I am following, I can make a significant contribution towards helping others. That is my purpose.

Every experience is a lesson, and it's up to me to discover the lessons and keep evolving. So right now, in this moment, I would answer yes. It's been an incredibly journey so far, and I am excited to see what is coming next!

About Sandra Fikus

Sandra Fikus is the owner of South Surrey Medical Clinic and Sereno Wellness and Spa. She was diagnosed with breast cancer ten years ago, and after completing years of treatment – which included eight surgeries, chemotherapy, radiation, a mastectomy and reconstruction – she discovered alternative ways to help herself through each recovery. Her first thought of opening a wellness center came to her while going through these treatments. Her vision has evolved into being an innovator in the medical and wellness field, specializing in women's health and using the latest technologies.

www.serenowellness.com
Email: Sandra@serenowellness.com
Instagram: Sereno Wellness & Spa, Sandra Fikus
Facebook: Sandra Fikus

12

FROM GRIEVING TO GROOVING

by Susan Marshall

"Twenty years from now you will be more disappointed by the things you didn't do than by the ones you did do. So throw off the bowlines, sail away from the safe harbor. Catch the trade winds in your sails. Explore. Dream. Discover."
H. Jackson Brown, Jr., "P.S. I Love You"

To my dear
Cousins Donna &
Vicki,
The travel bug must run in
our family as we all have it &
it's one of the most wonderful legacies
we could ever have. I love sharing
our travel experiences, ideas & tips
with each other & we always have so
much to talk about! Here's to happy,
safe and fun travels wherever the
globe takes us!

Love,
Cousin Sue

From Grieving to Grooving

by Susan Marshall

"Gee, Daddy, when I grow up, I want to go to Paris," my little girl's voice said to my dad, a pilot in the Royal Canadian Air Force who had just returned from a trip to France. He had given me a packet of little black and white photographs showing the Eiffel Tower, Arc de Triomphe, and Notre-Dame Cathedral. As I gazed at these photographs, the seed for my desire and passion to travel was planted. He had also recently been to Ghana when it achieved independence within the Commonwealth in 1957 and returned with a beautiful ebony carved figurehead for our home and a snakeskin wallet for me; I was intrigued by these unique souvenirs. He then told me he had flown Queen Elizabeth and Prince Philip over to attend the special Commonwealth ceremonies. Wow, my daddy was important!

My dad flew all over the world and wasn't home very much, leaving my mom with four little kids to look after. We were stationed at Air Force bases all over Canada so I was used to moving around. Sometimes it was challenging to get caught up in school as we were either way ahead or far behind, but we always managed. I grew up quite shy and naïve, like my friends were, even though we all bonded tightly to each other as "Air Force brats."

At this time, few women worked outside the home and were generally treated as "less than" and did as they were told. I remember being told once that girls shouldn't go to university because they just took the place of a boy and then left to have babies. There were only five career choices for women: secretary, nurse, teacher, airline stewardess, and banker. No such thing as an entrepreneur in those days, only a j-o-b! I wanted to be an airline stewardess but didn't have the required perfect eyesight, so I chose the secretarial career path instead.

As a teenager, all I ever talked about was going to Europe, to Paris. No marriage and babies for me, not for a long time! It was even written as my future goal in my Grade 12 yearbook: become an Executive Secretary, have my own car and go to Europe. After graduating from high school at the age of sixteen, I took a one-year Special Commercial Course and landed a great job at IBM's Head Office in Toronto. I had a brilliant career ahead of me, and after a short time I became an Executive Secretary. I had bought my own car by now, so the only thing left was to fulfill my goal of going to Europe.

When I was seventeen my girlfriend and I talked about taking a vacation to Nassau. This was a big deal because in the mid-60's girls just didn't take trips like that, especially to "exotic" places and especially without their parents. We booked a ten-day trip through a travel agent and ended up at a luxurious beachfront hotel. This was my first real taste of travel, and it whetted my appetite to see more of the world – especially more of those beaches and palm trees!

I then started dating a guy who was almost five years older than me and was attending university. I still wasn't interested in getting married as I really wanted to go to Europe first and see what the sights in those little black and white photographs really looked like. My boyfriend wanted to get married, though, and I relented because all my friends were getting married too. So at twenty, I became a bride. A bride who did as she was told, never spoke up, agreed with everything he said and did, and never realized she had her own voice. We never argued, of course, and I stifled any negative feelings. As with most people my age, I had been raised to be seen and not heard so I never learned how to express feelings of anger or conflict and just stuffed them down deep inside.

Shortly after we got married we decided to move out west to Vancouver, but were still busy saving our money so we could go to Europe first. In the early 70's, a lot of young people were going to Europe and Arthur Frommer's "Europe on $5 a Day" was the golden guidebook. Our plan was to travel for three months and lease a car from the factory in Paris. In the meantime, my husband had accepted a couple of local job transfers and fortunately I was able to transfer within IBM so I could keep working.

We finally arrived in Paris, and at last my dream had come true! We spent a week there, exploring and using our very limited French, staying in small pensions for yes, five dollars a day mostly! Paris was everything I had dreamed it would be and I was thrilled to be there. When we left the city to travel through Europe, our main staples became a loaf of bread, a hunk of cheese, and a 25¢ bottle of wine as we stopped often to have picnics along the roadside. Every country was a new experience, a new culture, a new language, a new currency, and a new lifestyle. I revelled in it all. Three months later we had put twenty-three countries under our belts. Every day I wrote meticulously in my diary, recounting each moment and detailing everything I saw. To this day, I can read the diary and relive the entire experience.

Once the trip finished, we headed back to Canada to pack up our belongings and head out West, our other big dream. Immediately I got a top job at IBM in Vancouver; however, my husband couldn't find the job he was looking for. After a couple of months he called me one day at work to tell me he found a position in Prince George, 500 miles north, and the decision was made. I gave up my career and reluctantly moved to a place where I was told the rates of divorce and alcoholism were the highest in Canada. I had never known anyone who was divorced and I didn't really drink, but I sure learned fast in this cold frozen frontier. Everyone drank, everywhere, and little did I know that I would leave nine years later, by myself with two little children.

During my time in Prince George, I experienced two miscarriages, the loss of my best friend to cancer, the forfeiture of my beautiful home because of the divorce, and winter weather at 40° below. After the divorce, I landed a fabulous fun job in festival management, travelled to Alaska twice, and further expanded my career. I eventually took assertiveness training which allowed me to grow both personally and professionally, and I became a founder of one of the Toastmasters Clubs.

When I was first on my own with my two little girls, I was scared and felt powerless and very hopeless. It took me a long time to heal from all my losses. However, I learned to do many things by myself; I had to in order for my family and I to survive. I had been laid off jobs more than once and eventually started working in the tourism and hospitality industries to feed my passion for travel and raise my daughters. These jobs enabled me to travel on business quite often, although I had to travel alone, eat alone, and attend many business functions alone as well.

I started spending my vacations in Mexico along with other single ladies I had met. I fell in love with the country – with the lifestyle, the people, and of course the margaritas and the sunshine too! Eventually I set up a marketing company to promote their resorts, which was fun but not financially viable. At this point I was struggling financially and had stood in the welfare lineup more than once.

After my eldest daughter left home, she decided to go to Australia and work for a year. I ended up joining her after spending the winter in Mexico. By now I had learned how to travel well on a budget so that I could stay in places longer. We ended up in Melbourne, where I cleaned the hostel in exchange for free nights, which I actually had fun doing! I was dating Aussie guys and having the time of my life. I even had an Aussie boyfriend who took me to Fiji, and to a beautiful resort where kangaroos were hopping around outside. He treated me very well, and my daughter said I should marry him and I would be set for the rest of my life. However, I didn't love him and at this point in my life I wasn't going to settle.

My daughter finally returned to Canada, and now I was totally on my own and it was time for me to move on. I headed up the coast with my trusty backpack and discovered I loved travelling solo while paying close attention to my tiny budget. I sailed in the Whitsundays, snorkelled in the Great Barrier Reef, hiked in the rainforest, and drove an Australian beach buggy. I then toured the north island of New Zealand, visited a Maori village, and experienced a cultural ceremony.

Next, I flew to Bali to meet a gal whom I had travelled with in Australia. We had an amazing time together, and after she left I took a rickety old boat to the tiny island of Lombok and just hung out. After that I flew to Singapore and enjoyed a Singapore Sling at the Raffles Hotel where the drink was made famous, toured throughout Malaysia, and stayed on a remote island in a hut with no electricity and snorkelled right from the beach for a couple of dollars. Being single all these years had prepared me well for travelling alone and meeting wonderful people along the way. I had evolved into being an adventurous world traveller, accompanied solely by my guidebook and my intuition, after acquiring the newfound life skills I had learned by being a single mom.

I carried on and eventually ended up in the Greek Islands, my ultimate destination. I had seen the movie "Shirley Valentine" in the early 90's and it left a big impression on me. I felt drawn to go to Mykonos where the movie was filmed. Unfortunately, I was out of money the night I arrived in Athens. I had just enough left to get myself home, so I was going to have to leave the next day. Thankfully I received an email that evening that a settlement from over a year ago had been reached with a hotel who had laid me off. I had filed a complaint against them for overtime, and now a very large cheque was being deposited into my bank account – talk about divine timing!

So off I went to explore the Greek Islands. The minute I walked into the Mykonos hotel movie site, I knew I was destined to bring women there to share the magic of the Greek Islands. I was able to stay there for three days at no cost in exchange for giving the owner marketing ideas to attract more business. I then toured six other islands over the next month, and every day was a new adventure! I learned as much as I could for future reference in order to put together an itinerary for my newly found passion. However, it would have to stay on the backburner for now as I had to get my finances in order.

I had been travelling for a year now, and it was time for me to return to Canada. I got my furniture and personal belongings out of storage and started working temp jobs to get back on my feet. My travels had all been worthwhile, but I yearned for more and celebrated the beginning of the new millennium in Mexico. I had always thought I'd like to retire in Mexico because I knew it so well and felt so comfortable there, like I could truly be myself. There is a casual, down-to-earth lifestyle that I feel as soon as I get off the plane.

In the early 2000's I was laid off yet another job and ended up spending the winter in Mexico with my severance package and taking an inexpensive tour through Belize and Guatemala. I loved every minute of it. I always felt confident and practiced my Spanish whenever I could. I knew how to travel well on a budget, staying at hostels and watching what I ate. If you travel with a positive attitude, an open mind, and always do your research, you're bound to have a good experience.

I started taking business and entrepreneurial courses, reading many books and networking with professionals. Having tried various network marketing businesses, I still hadn't found my little niche. By now, though, I knew that I wanted to do something on my own which involved travel.

Life then dealt me some really big losses. Besides battling health challenges with my thyroid, I lost my mom. A year later I also lost my dad, and then my younger sister passed away suddenly five months after him. I also lost all three uncles in the next couple of years, and two aunts had passed away just prior to them. I only have two aunts left now, both of whom are in their nineties and have dementia. After they go, I am the oldest in this generation. It's made me realize how fast life goes by, so I really want to live my life to the very fullest right now. There is only this very moment; there's never a guarantee that we will see tomorrow.

Since my tour of the Greek Islands, I knew that the time had now come to start my dream of putting together a tour there based on the movie "Shirley Valentine." Women all over the world still identify with the movie, and there are still many one-woman plays happening everywhere because of the impact this film has had. I knew this was my calling. However, I had to find a tour operator who would work with me. Over the course of two years, I went through five different tour operators. Yes, five! Each one ended up not having the same focus as I did for the tour; sadly, I had to put the tour on the back burner once more, another loss which I mourned deeply. But I never gave up!

One day I attended a travel show, and when speaking with a tour operator I casually mentioned my plan. She told me to send her my ideas, and she loved them! We were totally on the same page, so after several months of work the pieces are now finally coming together. We have organized a twelve-day tour through the Greek Islands which involves learning about ancient history, sightseeing, and relaxing under the Greek sun. During this tour, I will be putting on mini-workshops and exercises to help women grow, evolve, and recapture the essence of who they really are, buried underneath all the roles they might play of mother, grandmother, wife, employee, employer, entrepreneur, the list goes on. I feel it's my calling, my honour, and my passion to lead women on this enlightening journey.

My other dream, which I had discovered and buried years ago, was to retire in Mexico. Now this is happening too; I plan on spending my winters in the sunshine, mostly in Mexico but perhaps in other tropical places as well. I am creating a brand-new lifestyle and reinventing myself for the next chapter of my life. I realized that if I was going to live down south, I had to get rid of all my "stuff" that I had accumulated throughout the years. I started decluttering massive amounts of papers, magazines, books, ornaments, and stuff, stuff, stuff. It wasn't until I started that I realized how much there was. I began reading about minimalism, and even though I don't think I'll ever become a total minimalist I have certainly found homes for a lot of my things. Around this time a friend of mine had massive medical expenses, and I got the idea to sell all my stuff and do a fundraiser for her to help with the costs. It felt so good to be able to do this, and it was very rewarding from a spiritual standpoint too. At times it was a very painful journey as I beat myself up for accumulating so much and wasting money, but in the long run it was worth all the lessons I needed to learn.

I realized that life is too short to spend time grieving for losses of people or things and wallowing in painful memories, because we need to make the most of each precious moment we have on this beautiful earth. Being a single mom allowed me to develop the necessary skill set, resources, and passion to follow my dreams of travelling the world, having fun, and making a difference. I've graduated now from grieving to grooving!

Travel develops valuable character traits such as confidence and self-awareness; improves social and communication skills; broadens your horizons; enhances your tolerance for uncertainty, change, and different cultures and people; gives you a real-life education; and motivates you with a determination to succeed and overcome your fears. All of these can be applied to empowering women, as well as those around them, in our day to day lives.

It's a feeling of absolute freedom and inspiration which lingers in your mind and soul long afterwards. It's a voyage of the senses. Each morning, the rising sun brings a new promise as the day unfolds according to your desires. Tomorrow will be just as extraordinary. Away from home, you shed your skin and are born anew, curious and ready for adventure, open to whatever the day might bring, without plans or fears.

And for me, as the saying goes, "I'd rather have a passport full of stamps than a house full of stuff."

About Susan Marshall

Susan is a passionate world traveller and formed "Dreamweavers on the Go", an online presence dedicated to inspiring and motivating people to travel through shared real-life experiences. Her dad was a pilot in the Royal Canadian Air Force which labelled her as an "Air Force Brat," so she quickly became accustomed to moving. This led to her desire to learn more about the world and eventually she spent three months in Europe in the 70's, exploring twenty-three different countries. Her multifaceted career has included working as a travel consultant, special tourism projects manager, festival manager, tour guide, hotel sales director, marketing consultant, and executive secretary.

After raising two daughters by herself, she travelled the world for a year at the age of fifty-one. She had nothing but a backpack, a fistful of pennies, a peaceful heart, eyes and ears wide open, a "no fear" attitude, and a willingness to learn as much as she could about everywhere she went and everyone she met. With forty countries now tucked under her belt, her goal is to become a global volunteer, make a difference, and have fun.

Her interests include writing, yoga, meditation, natural health and wellness, reading, and spending quality time with her family and friends when she's not up in the air or under the ocean.

www.dreamweaversonthego.com
Twitter: @DreamWeaversOTG
Facebook: Dreamweavers On The Go

13

OPENING YOUR PANDORA'S BOX

by Dr. Nelie Johnson

"Shine the light of truth and self-knowledge into the dark places to bring understanding, dissolve fear, and find peace and healing."
Nelie C Johnson MD

Opening Your Pandora's Box

by Dr. Nelie Johnson

"I feel like quitting. I can't keep working this way." Hold on a minute. How could I be saying this to myself? I had invested eight years of university, a year of internship, and another four years of hospital training. How could I even consider walking away from my practice of family medicine?

It was the summer of 1991, ten years into my career, and I had been struggling with a growing sense of distress and frustration with my work. In the early years of my medical practice there was much that I enjoyed and appreciated being able to provide – helping my patients with their general health, getting them to urgent and specialist care as needed, supporting them through the tough times, and sharing in the joys and the pains.

However, I was meeting patients with conditions that I could not diagnose and with questions that I could not answer. More and more, I experienced the burden of my patients' demands to know what was wrong with them, wanting to be told what to do and asking for a pill to make them better. More and more, I felt I was skimming the surface of things, giving out band-aid solutions, not knowing how to – and not being able to – deal with the cause. I was left feeling frustrated and ineffective. I asked myself over and over: "what am I missing here?"

The seeds of my questioning and searching, however, actually began long before, in my final year of medical school. While studying for exams, I clearly recall a moment of reflection when I said to myself, "Medicine doesn't have all the answers. There are many healing traditions – homeopathy, herbology, naturopathy, Chinese medicine, ayurvedic medicine – that have made and continue to make contributions." Feeling overwhelmed by the immense variety of approaches, I very quickly put a lid on it and decided I had to start somewhere.

Some years later I read a book called "The Healing Arts: A Journey Through the Faces of Medicine" by Ted Kaptchuk and Michael Croucher, in which the authors travelled the world researching various healing traditions. The most profound message of the book for me came when the author asked a highly respected and venerable Traditional Chinese Medicine (TCM) practitioner whether he would favour TCM or Western Medicine if he was sick. The Chinese doctor's response went something like this: "They are both effective in different ways and both needed. They are like chopsticks and the bowl. Both are needed to eat your food. Where there is a single, clear dysfunction in body, such as heart attack, a bleeding emergency, or seizure, Western Medicine is like the chopsticks that can go in quickly and treat effectively. However, where the disease condition is less well-defined and involves several organ systems, then the subtler, gentler, more supportive approach of Chinese medicine (the bowl) is preferred." For me, this comment was stunning. It confirmed my own growing perspective that Western Medicine didn't have to have all the answers, and that there were many healing approaches that could work together synergistically.

However, with the daily pressures as a new doctor learning the art of medical practice, I forgot this perspective and came to feel the burden of being the doctor my patients sought to care for them and fix them. The more years I practiced, the more I realized what I didn't know. As close as I felt I was to being in the career of my choice, I was not happy. I began to feel more and more insignificant in my ability to make a difference to the health of my patients, especially so with my patients with cancer. Despite maximum therapy and even good results, they often returned to me in fear for their lives and I felt powerless to help.

I became so discouraged that I got to a point of saying I either had to get out of medicine or find something in my career that I could be really inspired and passionate about. Although I was seriously considering quitting, I knew that I was in no state to make such a major decision. I took a holiday, returned somewhat restored, and managed to shift my outlook enough to just accept that I was unhappy with my work. I put all my troubles "on the back burner" as it were, and focused on anything that made me feel good. By creating more play time and taking life less seriously, both personally and at work, I soon noticed I was smiling more and making jokes.

What happened next led to a breakthrough. In a whiff of insight, I realized that for quite some time I had been asking myself what I didn't like about my work. But what if I instead asked a different question: "What do I enjoy about my work?" Well, I liked counselling my patients in ways they could help themselves and advising them about health promotion. And then a single word floated into my awareness, coming up from the depths of my being, that I had not realized had been buried since medical school: "healing."

With that word, a rush of aliveness and tingling came over me. Eureka! That's it! That's what I want to be about. In that same moment, I realized I knew nothing about healing. I had never heard this word once in all my medical training, nor in any conversations with medical colleagues. I'd heard "cure" and "best outcome" but never "healing."

Rather than becoming discouraged, I allowed myself to not know and I asked for help. I very simply put out to the Universe, "Show me the small steps to healing for myself, so that I might show them to others." It became the mantra I would send out almost every day for months and years, and I waited. Very soon, Life began bringing me experiences for which no medical textbook or training had prepared me.

I went through an intense few months when I cared for and lost three patients to cancer. One was a young woman in her thirties with advanced colon cancer. I wasn't sure how to handle this situation, so I took a week-long course in palliative care which gave me more confidence with my medical skills. Once I had done all I could medically, I learned to let go of controlling the outcome. That was between my patient and her "God." In sitting with her, without having any textbook to tell me how, I discovered a place in me where I didn't have to do anything; one where I could simply be present and compassionate, holding a space of rest, of loving regard, for my patient and myself.

As I was moving through this period of my life, I remember asking myself why this was happening and what was I supposed to learn from this. Then I received the gift the experience with my patients had given me – to let go of the fear of facing cancer in others, along with my own sense of helpless, and to recognize that the quality of my presence with my patient was healing in and of itself. I learned that it was not so much what more I could do for my patients, but rather what more my patients could do for themselves.

I was now at a watershed in my career. I acknowledged the many advances and strengths of Medicine, but at the same time I knew it could not carry the entire load of the health of the patient. I now had the answer to my question, "what am I missing?" The answer was the patient. I realized Medicine was leaving out what patients knew – their own knowledge about how life events had affected them and about their emotional reactions, thoughts, and beliefs. Patients needed to be included as valued experts on their health care team.

I knew that in order to help my patients have better health outcomes and opportunities for healing, I needed to expand my perspective and approach to treating disease. I needed to look beyond the physical to the emotional, mental, and spiritual aspects as well. I needed to find a way to help my patients connect with both what was going on physically in their bodies and with what was going on internally in their daily lives – their thoughts, emotions, and beliefs. I needed a clear and indisputable understanding of what causes disease and what factors promote healing. And I needed to know what interventions or tools patients could use for their own healing. I could not be a healer for anyone but myself; however, I could be a guide and provide a structure of support and aids to help others along the way for their own healing and well-being.

Then, through a series of synchronicities, I found myself registered for an intensive 6-day course in Quebec City in the fall of 1997 – six years since my "aha" moment – which were given by a medical doctor from France named Claude Sabbah. He gave me the key piece I was missing: the link between emotional conflict and disease. This was a totally stunning breakthrough!

I learned that behind almost every illness and disease, there is an unresolved or partially resolved core emotional conflict or pattern of stress that is buried in the subconscious and out of the person's awareness. The disease is the outcome of the automatic or survival brain's drive to manage and contain this stress energy while maintaining the body/mind's best working capacity for as long as possible.

I learned that in reality, disease is a mechanism of survival. While maintaining the function of the organism as a whole, it gives the individual time to resolve the underlying conflict either 1) through an awakening awareness of the buried portion of the conflict and conscious effort to clear it, or 2) unconsciously, as in "time heals." I learned that every illness and disease carries a message. When one uncovers the message – the core issue involved – a direction for healing can open up.

I also learned that diseases and illnesses from colds to cancer operate similarly, the difference being in the intensity and duration of the stress pattern. In addition, I learned that every disease has two parts or phases: a conflict phase during which the person is caught up in stress, and a recovery phase after the conflict has been resolved when the body heals. I learned that different tissues and organs respond differently to stress. For example, when the glandular tissue of the breast is stressed, a growth will result. In contrast, the ducts of the breast show no tumour growth until the recovery phase, which then indicates the conflict has resolved and the tissue is repairing. Therefore, when a lump in the breast is diagnosed as cancer, it could indicate either that the woman is currently in a phase of stress in her life or that she is recovering from a period of high stress, depending on which part of the breast is involved.

Here's a case study of "Jennifer," who came to me seeking help. She had been diagnosed with intraductal breast cancer, and the unexpected shock threw her into a frenzy to get the cancer out. She had the lump removed within days and was then scrambling for any and every treatment that would rid her of the cancer completely.

Jennifer was totally blindsided by her diagnosis. She was very fit, maintained good nutrition, and practiced meditation. She was well-informed about natural health and believed herself to be emotionally and spiritually balanced. Despite how healthy she thought herself to be, she was struck with cancer. She felt her body had betrayed her.

In our first session, I explained to Jennifer that although the cancer seemed to have hit her randomly, there was an explanation as to why it had occurred at precisely this time in her life. Our job was to uncover the reason and the message that it carried. I asked her to set aside her focus on the cancer and bring her attention to the period of her life prior to the diagnosis. What were the dominant stresses and concerns in her life in the several months and years before?

The overriding concern for much of her adult life was a struggle with her marriage. She loved her husband, "Jake," but they were constantly arguing. They separated and came back together several times. Try as she might, she felt she failed to connect, communicate, and express the great love she had for him. Jennifer was frustrated and distressed with not being able to somehow make their marriage work.

Then came a period of several years of living apart, although they kept in touch with regards to their children. Conversations with Jake became more relaxed and Jennifer remained hopeful of a reconciliation. However, this possibility was dashed when Jake asked her for a divorce as he had found a woman he wanted to marry. Jennifer was shocked, upset, and very hurt. Her hopes of salvaging the marriage were shattered.

Jennifer was diligent in taking care of her physical and emotional health, and gradually the distress of the divorce faded. While life was good and she felt fairly calm and content, she remained deeply saddened and held onto some significant residual stress. What could she have done to save her marriage? If she had been more loving, forgiving, and understanding...

Just three or four months prior to discovering her cancer, a major shift occurred in Jennifer's life. She met a man with whom she experienced a very healthy and loving connection. As this relationship developed, she recognized that she was able to trust this man and express her vulnerability and love for him in a way she had never been able to do with her ex-husband. It was a relief and a joy for her to finally make this level of connection with her new partner, and this relationship opened up a wonderful phase in her life. How could her diagnosis possibly happen precisely when her life was opening to a greater level of joy, happiness, and depth of relating than she had ever felt before?

Working with me to explore her story, Jennifer came to appreciate and understand the full impact of the struggle in her marriage with Jake. Biologically, this emotional stress manifested in her body by infinitesimally expanding her breast ducts in order to deliver more "milk" at the nipple to strengthen her connection with him. She did not fully let go of the conflict until after she met the new man in her life. As a result of this positive shift, her survival brain read a complete drop of stress energy around this core issue, which then initiated the recovery phase resulting in "tumour" growth. The ducts of her breast were able to repair through a rapid growth of tissue, which showed up as a mass in her breast.

However, the mass was temporary and would dissolve on its own, similar to what happens with the healing of a bone fracture. In a fracture, a callous – which is a bony mass or lump of healing tissue – forms a cuff around the damaged bone. When the fracture is sufficiently healed, this extra tissue dissolves to restore the normal outline of the bone.

Now the "cancer" made sense to Jennifer. She was greatly relieved that the tumour had not appeared out of the blue, but instead matched exactly the emotional pattern in her life. She was able to release much of her fear and confusion and felt more confident in her treatment choices going forward, knowing that she had cleared the emotional root cause of the cancer.

After having the lump removed she had consulted two oncologists, the first of whom had recommended chemotherapy and radiation. In the opinion of the second oncologist, however, she did not require chemo and radiation as all the cancer had been removed by surgery. However, she could consider relapse prevention therapy with Tamoxifen. Jennifer was greatly relieved to receive the second opinion as she was not at all comfortable with taking chemo or submitting to radiation. She tried Tamoxifen, did not tolerate it, and stopped taking it.

As of November 2017, Jennifer has been living well, is continuing to grow emotionally and spiritually, and has been cancer free for eight years now. In a recent phone conversation, she shared that she had been more afraid of the chemo and radiation than the cancer. From her experience, she learned that her doctors could advise her on the treatment options, but ultimately the choice and the responsibility for her healing journey belonged to her.

There is no one path to healing. Jennifer only had surgery, while others choose to do all possible medical treatments. I request that patients keep seeing their doctors and continue therapies they find supportive and helpful, along with doing whatever they can to clear the emotional stress patterns. When emotional healing is combined with medical and other therapies, they can work together to improve outcomes.

For complex illnesses, neurodegenerative and neurodevelopmental diseases, or health conditions with no clear diagnosis that have multiple causes – such as when nutritional deficiencies or excesses, food allergies or sensitivities, environmental toxicity, or genetic predisposition are found to be contributing factors in dementia, Parkinson's, Lyme disease, autism, chronic fatigue syndrome, MS, and depression to name a few – a comprehensive approach involving proper nutrition, lifestyle changes, detoxification, and stress and sleep management is required. However, even in these cases, for some individuals emotional stress maybe the dominant cause. For example, I have helped a patient to heal fully from fourteen years of pain, fatigue, and depression from chronic fatigue syndrome in a few months by supporting her to access and let go the associated emotional conflicts.

Throughout this chapter I have touched on several moments of learning and wisdom that I have gained by shining light into my dark places. Let me summarize a few key lessons:

1. For deep down happiness and fulfillment, find out what inspires you, what you really care about, and how you want to make a difference in the world.

2. When you feel lost and stuck, accept how you are feeling and don't fight it. Give yourself a time out and take the pressure off – go play, do things that nurture and relax you, have fun, and surprise yourself with what shows up to help

you feel less lost and more free. It might be one idea, one small step, or, as in my case, one word.

3. Pay attention to the questions you ask yourself, as the quality of the question affects the quality of your answer. Frame the question in a way that directs you to what you want and how you want to be and feel rather than what you don't want. One powerful question is "what can I learn from this?"

4. Be willing to think outside the box and to look at things differently.

5. Give priority to your self-care and make use of whatever contributes the most to your ease, relaxation, peace of mind, and joy. To be able to continually serve and give generously, you have to fill and refill yourself first.

6. Be willing to share your experience and wisdom. You never know how many people your story might touch, inspire, and help along a path to better health, well-being, and personal transformation.

Behind many illnesses and diseases, it is possible to uncover a hidden emotional story. Disease becomes the physical metaphor or representation of a pattern of conflict held subconsciously, out of the person's full awareness. The disease is showing up for a reason and carries a message. Healing is enhanced when this message is brought into one's awareness and acted upon to clear conflict and restore a state of well-being. For me the key to dealing with cancer, or any illness, is to understand why it is showing up rather than fearing and fighting it.

Have the courage and be willing to open your "Pandora's box" of feelings so you can heal. Know yourself to be your very own healer and the power in your life for health and joy.

Wishing blessings, courage, health, joy, and peace to all.

About Dr. Nelie Johnson

Ever asked yourself or wondered "why am I sick?" or "is my body trying to tell me something?" or "why do patterns keep repeating in my life?" The answer to these questions is what fascinates Dr. Nelie. Her passion is to help people find their own answers and create possibilities for greater health and happiness.

As a family physician for over thirty years who is trained in mind-body-emotional healing, she brings a breadth of knowledge and experience to every private or group encounter. She has a special interest in helping women facing breast cancer to move past fear and despair toward understanding and empowerment in their own healing and well-being. She has produced a DVD, entitled "It's Time to Heal Breast Cancer - going from surviving to healing," to support them.

At a time when there is much fear around cancer and other diseases, Dr. Nelie has much good news to share. In 2010 she was the creator and co-organizer of the May 1st Forum "It's Time to Heal," which explored an expanded disease model and an integrative approach to treating illness. She was also a presenter along with Dr. Bruce Lipton, internationally known author of "The Biology of Belief" and expert on the impact of thoughts, emotions and beliefs on physiology.

A proud second-generation Vancouverite, Dr Nelie is

an avid traveller and active outdoors woman. She is most appreciative of the healing balm of time spent in nature.

Dr Nelie is currently writing a book. She welcomes you to contact her for private consultations and speaking engagements.

www.awarenessheals.ca
Phone: 604-467-1794
Email: nelie@awarenessheals.ca
Facebook: DrNelieJohnson

14

INVEST IN YOUR BIRTHRIGHT OF LIFE

by Karen Angelucci

"Wake up all the desire and pleasure that your body is capable of experiencing, let your past go, and follow your bliss just for the health of it."
Dr. Christiane Northrup

Invest in Your Birthright of Life

by Karen Angelucci

Many of us have our woe story, and like many others mine includes dysfunctional family, injuries that caused pain and difficulty with movement, and a sense of disconnection within myself. I started working when I was sixteen, got married at eighteen, and thought I was grown up because I was marrying a man who was ten years older than me. Not having life skills, relationship skills, or communication skills caught up with me in my late twenties, which then tore my life apart before becoming my resource for change in my early forties.

My early working years were spent as a food clerk, a legal secretary, and doing trust accounting for law firms. Late into my twenties I became a mom and worked part-time as a self-employed bookkeeper, and then in my early thirties I became a single mom. Needing a full-time job, I started working as the administrator for a small real estate development company to support my daughter and I. The job had flexible hours, which allowed me to attend my daughter's school functions, and I was able to pay my bills.

Being in a small office meant I spent my working hours alone; the owner was often out making deals, and the project manager and the other employees were at the construction site. Sitting at my desk, however, was becoming uncomfortable. Years earlier I had fallen six feet from the deck of a sailboat, landing on my tailbone on the hard wooden edge of a bench inside the galley and bouncing onto the floor. The lasting effects from this injury were causing me physical distress, and along with the need to be more active I also wanted more social engagement in my work.

I approached my employer and had a heart-to-heart talk about advancing in the company by taking on more of a PR role. His answer made my jaw drop: "You need to have a penis to do that." There was no sexual overtone to his comment, just pure masculine righteousness. Up until now I had noticed that men and women were given different roles and responsibilities in the workplace, and I had been okay with that. However, hearing these words spoken by my employer ignited a fire within me to have my own path in career and life, even if I didn't know what that looked like yet.

This was the beginning of a period of change for me. With each new door I was willing to open came the opportunity to explore, become more curious, feel inspired to grow, and take steps to build trust and confidence in myself.

Motivation, apathy, crisis, curiosity, inspiration, serendipity…all of these have been an impetus for change in my career and my life choices.

In the 1950's, when I was a kid, self-care wasn't a

consideration. My mom would ask me to walk on her back or bring her crackers in bed because her migraines were so bad. I felt helpless. I had no comprehension of the distress her body was in, and it wasn't until after my fall that I began to recognize how pain could alter the way I moved or create dysfunction for years to come. Growing up seeing my mother's physical and emotional pains became a motivating force for the choices I made in my life and career.

In my late twenties I began feeling a sense of disconnection and apathy within my marriage. Couples counselling introduced me to weekend retreats where I attended self-development workshops. While ultimately my husband and I separated when my daughter was two, choosing to learn about myself through these self-development courses laid the foundation I needed to change my life and became my path to a new career. As a result, my woe of physical and emotional stressors from my injury and dysfunction became my springboard to a win.

As I learned to resource my body's signals and messages, I gained a vocabulary to communicate my feelings, to trust, to give and receive, and to be in relationship with myself and others. My body was talking and I was learning to listen.

I knew I needed to attend to the dysfunction and pain I was experiencing from the fall and the emotional turmoil in my life. It wasn't always easy; some of the doors I opened uncorked effervescent bubbles of emotions, while others were like volcanic eruptions. However, my commitment to self-discovery and self-compassion always guided me to safe places.

When I was attending the retreats, I was introduced to a movement class called Contact Improvisation. Participating in this class opened deep wounds of self-judgment and lovingly directed me to the Pilates method of exercise. In the late 1980's, this type of exercise was still very new and relatively unknown;

when I told people what I was doing, they thought I was going for pie and a latte! But as soon as I started I knew it was what my body needed and wanted. I began making connections in my body that helped me be strong.

After taking classes for over a year, I approached the owner of the Vancouver studio and asked what it would take to become an instructor. There was no certification training at that time; instead, everything was done under supervision in the studio. I was accepted, and this started deepening my journey of learning about my body. Inspired by the people around me and the positive changes I was experiencing, I began studying other self-care modalities and going to integrative health practitioners. This was the community I was looking for.

As I was on the path to becoming an instructor, Pilates was becoming more well-known and certification training courses were developed, which I completed in 1995. I was teaching part-time at the studio in Vancouver and part-time out of my home in South Surrey, which allowed me to be an active parent to my free-spirited teenage daughter. In 1996 I was approached by a physiotherapist to open a studio in her clinic, and the Bodytalk Pilates Studio in my home moved to become the first Pilates practice affiliated with a physiotherapy clinic in Western Canada.

Working in the clinic was an amazing opportunity. If I was working with a client that had a dysfunctional movement pattern, I would ask a physiotherapist to see them and go with the client to view the treatment. When the client returned I could see the improved movement pattern. This excited me and made me want to know more about anatomy.

Over the years I had heard about something called Osteopathy and I was curious about what it offered. I knew nothing about the practice, and when I made inquiries online, it appeared that the only training available was in Europe or Eastern Canada. Thankfully this new door was serendipitously opened for me in 2010, when a colleague of mine hosted a workshop by an instructor from Toronto about combining techniques from Pilates and Osteopathy.

As I arrived at the workshop, a woman was unlocking the door next to the studio. I then noticed that the sign on the door read "Osteopath clinic." When I asked her where she trained, she told me that The Canadian College of Osteopathy had a satellite college in Vancouver that was affiliated with the head office in Montreal. I couldn't find the information before because the website was all in French and I didn't think to translate it to English! I went home from the workshop and immediately made inquiries to apply to the college. Luckily they accepted my years of work experience as a Pilates practitioner, along with the modalities I studied and my connection with a physiotherapist, and allowed me to enroll in the five-year part-time course. I started the program in the fall of 2010 and WOW, was I in the right place to learn anatomy!

Osteopathy in Canada is a practice requiring in-depth understanding of the body in order to implement specific techniques. The manual treatments are used to release tissue tensions with the intent of restoring the body's innate ability to heal. What that means is that "We Heal from the Inside Out"! Through my studies, I have learned that our ability to move on a daily basis is not as simple as muscles moving bones and that injuries or surgeries may affect more than just the trauma site. Osteopathy helped me look deeper at the source of dysfunctions or pain and realize that the body's healing capacity can be nurtured by the release of the strains often caused by injuries, surgeries, falls, accidents, improper movement patterns, and emotional stressors. Our body has amazing capacity to compensate in an attempt to accommodate our "just do it" style of thinking; until we learn to take care of our body in ways that keep us strong and thriving, it will degenerate from misuse, misalignment, disease, and neglect. Prevention and early intervention are much better strategies for ensuring the longevity of your most crucial asset!

We all have a body. We experience our world through our senses, and our body is our mode of transport that supports our movement as we manifest our deepest urges or desires. When the interpretation of our senses gets skewed with pain, anger, or other harsh environments, our quality of life is diminished. Exploring your senses offers new and delicious opportunities to rediscover ways of being. I am fascinated how each of us interprets the experience of this magical and mysterious kaleidoscope of life, and I want to help people create a healthy body and a feeling of zest for life.

I continue to teach Pilates in my fully-equipped studio, which I have now combined with the substantial tool kit of manual techniques I learned in Osteopathy, and I have branched out to teaching groups in the community. In my private practice I work with individuals to manually release areas in the body that are often the underlying causes of their aches and pains, or that are contributing to degenerative conditions which are passed off as just "getting older." Clients are also taught self-release techniques tailored to their needs. As physical or emotional dysfunctional patterns are released, they work to build strength with exercises and develop flexibility with stretches. Depending on the person's needs, I may refer them to other resources or practitioners which will support their health and well being.

I am in awe of the human body and I appreciate how it responds when given what it needs. The difficulty is that we all have specific health needs that require personalized answers.

Through my years as a Pilates practitioner and my ongoing studies in Osteopathy, it has become clear to me that everyone should be empowered in making their own health care choices. I want to help people reduce the struggle, fear, or confusion about what to do for themselves and who to go to for assistance. To meet this need, I created my company Birthright Investment which includes my private practice, group teaching workshops, and speaking engagements. The eleven-module workshop series I developed is experiential, which allows you to explore new ways of thinking about your body and opens you to new feelings and ways of being. The expansion of my private practice into workshops has allowed me to have a greater reach in teaching people about the links in their physical functions. Participants learn to be responsive to the signals and symptoms they experience and to understand the available practices which can support their path to personalized health care.

I come to the table with over twenty years of experience helping people understand where to put their time and energy in order to get results, as well as how to release dysfunctional patterns related to the physical, emotional, and nutritional functions of the body. Through implementing this self-discovery paradigm, you create new experiences that rewrite your story and prevent you from getting trapped in the excuse of old age. As said by Dr. Christiane Northrup, a leading authority in women's health and wellness, "The way you're living your life right in the present moment and the beliefs with which you're living your life are creating your cells day to day." Actions today create the cells of the future.

REAL HEALTH NEEDS REAL ANSWERS and discovering your personal path is key. Each of us has our own resources and understanding to work with, along with a lot of confusion about what our body needs to function in good health. It's important to recognize what works for you and develop the skills to attend to your needs, as well as drawing on the resources of the medical and integrative practices that can support you.

Discovering the relationship between healing the body, the family, the community, and beyond is the essence that skilled practitioners offer to transition us out of struggle, vulnerability, and challenges that block, inhibit, or cripple us. Is your body sending you signals of pain and suffering, and telling you to make changes? How depleted are you willing to let yourself get before you take action to support and care for yourself? These questions are difficult to answer on our own at times and are opportunities to seek solutions from others; this is where practitioners are essential. Each individual is unique, and I think learning about your body and health care choices is empowering and vitally important.

Your body is an amazing resource – it is a guide that informs you what is important and what you value, and your Birthright of Life! It is a vessel to manifest your heart's desire and a vehicle for you to take action and to experience being, regardless of the circumstances.

I share my Birthright of Life with reverence and in honour of three influential relationships which directed my choices and gave me opportunities to create my life path: my body, my mother, and my daughter.

Through My Body, I found my voice and the words to communicate how I feel, think, and relate.

My Mother, through her inability to voice her needs, taught me the importance of valuing what is important to me and sewing this into my life every day. When she was 102, I asked her if she was happy or sad, and her answer was that she was empty. Knowing yourself doesn't happen at the end of life, it happens every day. Take time to care about yourself; if you don't, who will?

My Daughter Adera is the beacon of light that has taught me to see, both internally and externally, how our energy and excitement for life is renewed when we step out of our comfort zone. She has helped me overcome my fears and do things I never thought possible.

For example, up until my thirties I had a fear of touching other people. To this day I don't know what caused it, whether it was being the youngest in the family, feeling like an only child, withdrawing into the solitude of self-reliance, lack of communication skills, or who knows what else. However, I was okay giving Adera a back rub at night to send her into dreamland feeling comfort and care. In my late thirties, Adera said to me, "Mom, you should do this for a living." *Huh, weird*, I thought. Shortly afterward a friend commented, "You should do massage, you have such a nice touch." I had been taking Touch for Health classes and was practicing muscle testing on her, and she felt people would understand massage much better which would make it a good way to introduce the muscle testing. Touch for Health is based on the meridians of acupuncture, which I found intriguing; this led to studying Shiatsu as a form of massage related to these meridians and adding Swedish massage to the mix. I then bought a portable table and started doing house calls to supplement teaching Pilates part-time. Interesting how seeds of encouragement can alter the fears we have about ourselves.

As a practitioner, I help people feel good and trust their body. I invite you to join the community of service that your heart calls you to support. Your life experience, wisdom, or trauma that served as a catalyst for your changes can also serve others, because you know the steps you took and the benefits to taking action. Applying this can be a career calling or simply a personal sharing. Through the experiences and observations I have had while working with people, I have discovered that finding the path to being healthy requires you to be an active participant. The sooner you get started, the longer you'll get to enjoy the results. The shortcut is taking action NOW instead of thinking that someone else is going to fix you. Your body is miraculous when it comes to healing. A practitioner opens the door and provides information to help you restore balance in your body, but it is how you nurture this opening of self-discovery that leads you to health recovery. Leaning into aspects of my life that were physically and emotionally painful at the time actually opened the doors to working in a career that teaches me about my body and allows me to share this knowledge with others.

My journey to learning and creating my entrepreneurial path has been to unite my love of physical movement, Osteopathy, and my personal experiential path. I started working with thinking this is what I have to do, was then guided by what I needed to do, and now I am embracing my heart's desire. I want to share in the "AHA" excitement of helping you reclaim your body so you are out exploring, sharing, and thriving in your business and your life. I am your cheerleader, helping you to turn off your body struggles and turn on your innate healing.

Cheers to YOU; cheers for taking initiatives for your health; cheers for defining your path to thrive.

About Karen Angelucci

Karen's experiences of tuning in to her physical sensations became a resource of information for her evolution. A level of communication with herself and others developed because she began listening to her body to help her understand who she is and what's important to her!

Karen's curiosity about the human body drives her passion. Having worked with clients individually and in workshops for over twenty years, she helps people develop their self-help skills in order to attend to their body and find the practitioners they need to support their wellbeing.

She has learned it's possible to open the door to healing from the inside out. She recognizes the benefits of investing in herself and embraces the magic and mystery of living fulfilled in the life that she has been gifted with.

Karen was Pilates Certified in 1995 and over the years taken classes in many modalities of self-care. She combines these with skills learned in Osteopathic studies in her private practice. She continues to expand her circle of influence to include workshops and speaking engagements where she teaches you how to resource the information your body offers to you, realize what's important to you, understand what you value, and communicate this to the world.

Karen wants to embolden you to learn about your body,

educate you about how to make choices to care for your body, and inspire you to take action and invest in your birthright of physical, emotional, and nutritional health and well-being.

www.birthrightinvestment.com
Email: hello@birthrightinvestment.com
Facebook: Karen Angelucci or birthrightinvestment

$\overline{15}$

THE UNBRIDLED SOUL

by Krista Brown

"I think midlife is when the universe gently places her hands upon your shoulders, pulls you close, and whispers in your ear: I'm not screwing around. It's time."
Brene Brown

The Unbridled Soul

by Krista Brown

It starts as a low rumble, like a herd of a thousand distant hooves galloping toward you from over the horizon. Growing louder until eventually you feel the earth beneath your feet begin to move. It's an unsettling yet oddly exhilarating force of nature. A power unto itself, designed to shake things up and awaken you to a deeper soul calling.

What is it about midlife that profoundly re-shapes the well-worn path of our lives? That creates a distinct threshold for change? For some women it may be a change from being a full-time hands-on mom to an empty nester as her children find their wings and begin life on their own. For others there might be the catalyst of a death, a serious illness, a relationship break-up, or a job loss. And for others still, it may simply be the passage of time marked by a significant birthday and the realization that we're at the midway point, or beyond. Time no longer feels infinite.

Whatever the impetus, this midlife phenomenon is showing up in something called the Happiness U-curve. It turns out that economists have been studying people's happiness factor since the 1970's, and their results show that life satisfaction typically declines with age for the first couple of decades in adulthood until they bottom out somewhere in the forties or early fifties, and then increase again in the latter years.

During this time, we're naturally drawn inward as the foundation of our carefully crafted life begins to falter. Finding ourselves perched on the edge of something unknown and unfamiliar, deep existential questions begin to arise - who am I? Beyond my role as mother, wife, daughter, sister, friend, and colleague, who am I really? What is the deeper meaning of my life? Is this all there is? Do I have a deeper purpose? If so, what is it?

This is the journey I unexpectedly found myself on not long after the calendar had turned on my forty-first year. A journey that, by its very nature, felt wildly destructive as it called into question everything I had so carefully spent the last twenty years building. The stigma associated with what has come to be known as a "midlife crisis" sent me into hiding. What would people think? Aren't I supposed to have it all together by now? Why was I not feeling fulfilled? It was a lonely and confusing time as I navigated the broken pieces of a life I had seemingly outgrown. Feeling ashamed, battered, and lost, I cocooned myself away from family and friends. I immersed myself in self-help books, healing retreats, and spiritual teachings looking for guidance. What I would come to realize is that this "crisis" was in fact an awakening to a deeper aspect of myself, seeking fulfillment beyond the material gains our society places so much value on.

An Unlikely Teacher

An unlikely teacher and healer had entered my life during these changing times. A teacher sporting a long flowing mane and tail, four hooves, and wise eyes that seemed to see right into my soul. Little did I know then that my introduction to horses was about to set my life on a whole new trajectory.

Having grown up in suburbia, I had no real experience with horses. But now, decades later, as I settled in to full-time practice as a Homeopath, I was searching for a hobby that would offer me some respite from the hours and hours of case study. "What about horses," my husband casually suggested one day. "You love animals and the outdoors." "I don't know the first thing about horses," I was quick to counter. But there was something in that brief exchange that took root in me, and I soon approached a co-worker whom I knew to be a rider with the idea of learning how to ride. I explained to her that I had no prior experience with horses and didn't even know where to start. She graciously agreed to take me to her barn and introduce me to their riding coach; thus began my journey into the wonderful world of horses.

I can still vividly recall my first day entering the barn. Walking down the center aisle with my arms pressed close to my sides, ensuring I was safely out of reach of the many curious faces peering over their stall walls. I had never been this close to such a big animal before and I knew nothing of their temperament. And yet, there was something warmly intoxicating about being in their presence.

Twice a week thereafter I would escape to the barn and learn to groom, tack and ride these majestic creatures. Hours would pass by unnoticed as the outside world and all its demands seemed to fade away. It wasn't long before my intended hobby grew into an all-consuming passion. Learning to ride was thrilling, but moreover I was drawn in by the soul of these sentient beings. Their gentle sensitivity, contrasted by a thousand pounds of unbridled power. Their willingness to carry us upon their backs. Their uncanny ability to read us.

It was only a couple of years into my new hobby that I learned about a new and growing field employing horses as teachers and guides in the areas of healing and transformation. As the foundations of my own life began to shift and change, I was drawn to explore this field more deeply. I attended a weekend retreat which seemed to awaken me to a deeper aspect of myself; my wiser and more intuitive self. The self who was seeking a voice during these changing times.

By this time I had acquired my very first horse: a 16.2hh handsome and gregarious gelding named Romeo, and true to form, a real ladies man! He would become one of my life's greatest teachers. Not long after I decided to become a trained facilitator in the area of healing and transformation through partnering with horses, called Equine Assisted Learning. In many respects, the experiential nature of the training became my own therapy. Instead of sitting in a counselling office trying to cognitively sort through the pieces of my life, I stood outside in a roundpen next to my chosen horse partner and silently connected my heart to hers. With her patient and non-judgmental guidance, I would navigate the depths of my body and soul seeking answers to the deep existential question – who am I?

Each time I entered the space with a horse I was invited to look deeper within myself for those answers. If I wanted to connect with the horse, I first needed to connect with myself; all aspects of myself. If I wanted to be in relationship with this horse, I had to deepen my awareness around what I was bringing to that relationship.

As an animal who is naturally preyed upon in the wild, the horse has developed a highly sophisticated ability to sense emotional energy as a means of survival. Their life is dependent upon their ability to accurately read the intentions of a predator, a herd mate, or the people who share their space. In order for the horse to feel safe in our presence, we must align to the truth of who we are and how we are feeling. We need to recognize when we are feeling sad, scared, confused, angry, or anxious, and allow ourselves to experience those emotions. This is a rather foreign concept in our increasingly disconnected society that encourages busyness and distraction as a way of numbing ourselves to unwanted emotions. But it is here, with our emotions, where we begin to meet ourselves.

One of the most profound experiences I have ever witnessed with a client was with a woman we'll call Beth. Beth came seeking support as she transitioned out of her marriage. She always considered herself to be the "strong one" but admitted to feeling overwhelmed with her current situation. Yet she was determined to "work through it as quickly as possible and move on!"

Beth entered the arena with her chosen horse guide, both free to move around at liberty. After walking in a large circle, the horse made her way back to Beth, dropped to the ground, and rolled over onto her back. I explained to Beth that as an animal who is naturally preyed upon in the wild, she was putting herself in a very vulnerable position by lying down and exposing her belly. I invited Beth to reflect on how this may relate to her current situation. As Beth quietly pondered, the horse returned to her feet and blew-out a release of tension through her nose. Beth nodded her head and, with a resigned smile, gave voice to the message she saw reflected in the horse's vulnerability - "release and surrender." Over the course of Beth's session, the horse would repeat this message three times! A very poignant reminder that sometimes we are being asked to release and surrender to life's process, rather than trying to push our way through it and move on.

Beth walked toward the center of the arena and then turned her attention back toward the horse; as if right on cue, the horse erupted into a gallop, encircling Beth at safe distance as she bucked and kicked into the air. After a couple of rounds she came to rest a good distance away from Beth, winded and trying to catch her breath. There was a momentary pause before Beth took a couple of tentative steps toward the horse and watched as once again she erupted into a flurry of galloping bucks and kicks. At that moment Beth looked at me and said, "that's what it feels like inside – like a tornado," as she gestured towards her heart. I invited her to acknowledge and embrace the tornado inside so the horse no longer had to mirror it for her. "Bring your awareness into your body," I urged her, "and acknowledge the tornado. Let yourself feel the emotion." Tears sprang from Beth's eyes, and the horse's body posture softened, lowering her head and blowing-out another release of tension before quietly walking toward Beth. Together they stood in quiet reflection; the horse stood with her head positioned at Beth's solar plexus, holding gentle, sacred space for her as she fully aligned with the truth of her emotions.

Unlike us, horses don't judge feelings to be "good" or "bad." They simply use feelings as information. Once Beth was able to let her guard down and acknowledge and express how she was truly feeling, the horse felt comfortable enough to stand in her presence. From this authentically aligned space we can access the clarity and answers we seek on our life's journey. In Beth's case, her new awareness led her to a year of travelling the world, listening to, and honouring, the deeper callings of her soul and finally settling into her passion as a healer.

Like Beth, it was in the company of horses where I deepened my experience of who I am; where I began to understand the deeper meaning of my life and, more poignantly, the significance of the changing times I found myself in. Change awakens us to a deeper calling. In my case, it was a calling that would take me from my comfortable suburban life to the adventures of farming, learning to work the land, and raising horses. A calling that would see me trade in my office attire for jeans and cowboy boots.

Pain Pushes Until the Vision Pulls

Alongside my journey with horses, I continued on my path of self-discovery and I began to explore the healing opportunities of group retreats. On one particularly memorable retreat, the seed for my own retreat center and my new entrepreneurial business was planted.

It was a brilliantly sunny June day in the French Alps, and I sat perched atop the stone wall of an old repurposed monastery where a group of international seekers had gathered on a week-long retreat. We were on a midday break after an intense morning of process work and I had taken my cup of freshly harvested wild thyme tea outside and found a spot on the wall to sit and take in the view of the surrounding snow-capped mountains. The mostly barren landscape was a perfect setting to reflect and contemplate the deep inner work we had gathered here to do.

As I sat in reflection, I was suddenly deeply struck by the awareness of the illusion of separation we ordinarily live under and how it shapes our life experiences. Our group was a mix of women and men from diverse cultural backgrounds, with our ages spanning three decades; outside of this retreat, we may not have ever had the opportunity to meet or relate to each other. But when we gathered in this sacred space to heal and to transform through the sharing and witnessing of our stories, we were able to witness aspects of our self in each other regardless of gender, age, or cultural differences, and to see through that illusion. For the first time, I no longer felt alone on this journey.

In that moment, I decided that I must find a way to bring this into my work. A safe space for people to gather, away from the daily distractions of their busy lives, and completely immerse themselves in the deeper callings of their soul. A place where we can come together and lay bare the frailties of our shared human experience in support of one another on this journey through life. And with that, I could feel the larger vision begin to pull. A tranquil retreat center set amongst old growth trees and expansive pasture land, where my herd of horses could welcome and guide those who are on their own personal path of discovery.

My husband welcomed the idea of new adventures and we began our property search. A search that would span many months and include everything from bare parcels of land, to old "fixer uppers," to finally the call that would set my vision in motion. Our realtor had found a property for sale just minutes from where we lived. "I think it really fits with your vision, but," he said hesitantly, "it's a little outside of your budget." Well, it couldn't hurt to look, could it?

It was perfect, almost as if it had been set up just for us. A large beautiful barn boasting a stunning finished loft space, offering the perfect setting for workshops and retreats. A delightful older farmhouse that needed just a few updates to embody that country-chic charm I was after, with luxurious accommodations and the warmth of home for intimate group gatherings. All set on acres of private lush greenspace with old growth trees and expansive pasture land for the horses.

This was it! This was the home of my future retreat center. Of course, we still had the issue of the enormous price tag. But I knew I hadn't been guided this far to give up now. I looked skyward and said, "Okay Universe, if this is where I am meant to be then make it happen." And it did. Supported by a motivated seller who dropped their asking price and an equally motivated buyer who purchased our home for more than its estimated value, we became the new owners of what has come to be known as Wisteria Acres Wellness & Retreats

Three more horses would join us on the farm – Cassi, Cricket and Rayne – growing our herd to four.

The learning curve that came with running a farm, raising horses, and operating a retreat center has been steep, but it has always been steeped in passion and purpose.

I recall a conversation I had with my mother one day not long into this new journey. Surprised by the rather unconventional and somewhat drastic change in my life's path, she asked "where did this come from?" "I have no idea," I replied, "all I know is it feeds my soul." I am, perhaps, as surprised as anyone to find myself on this path. It's not one I could have foreseen, yet this is where my soul has lead me and where I find deep meaning and a sense of purpose in my everyday life, whether I'm making my early morning trek to the barn on a frosty winter's day to feed my herd or guiding a client on their own personal journey of discovery on a warm summer's afternoon.

What My Path Has Taught Me About Embracing Change

When change beckons, whether at midlife or any other stage, greet it with an open and curious heart. Welcome the opportunity to discover new frontiers, fuel new passions, cultivate new skills and birth new dreams. Take time to hold space for the soft voice within through meditation, immersing yourself in nature, journaling, or sharing sacred space with a horse guide. Notice what lights you up, and conversely what weighs you down. Listen to the messages your body is sending you through feelings, sensations, or symptoms and be courageous enough to follow their wisdom. Be bold and brave in the pursuit of what makes your soul happy and gently let go of anything that no longer fulfills you.

It oftentimes means standing poised on the edge of everything that feels comfortable and familiar and courageously following the intuitive nudge to leap into the unknown, trusting you will be given wings to fly. And you will, because after all you are a part of a greater plan, a higher source, and an infinite wisdom. You are more than your physical body, more than your personality, your intellect, your ego, and all the limited beliefs they hold. Your purpose here in this life extends far beyond your roles, your relationships, your job, or any material wealth you could accumulate. You are greater than your circumstances, your pain, and your fears. You are a soul seeking its own evolution through all of these aspects.

It's time to live unbridled.

About Krista Brown

As *"lead mare"* at Wisteria Acres Wellness & Retreats and The Unbridled Soul, Krista partners with her herd of horses to guide those who are called to explore the deeper callings of their soul at her retreat center just outside Vancouver, British Columbia, Canada. As an intuitive Life Coach and Equine Guided Facilitator, Krista is passionate about supporting and empowering her clients to be courageous and powerful co-creators of their lives.

Krista offers online coaching services for those unable to join her at her retreat center as well as in-person private horse wisdom sessions, group workshops, and private or group retreats. She also welcomes groups, offering meditation, yoga, healing, self-development, corporate retreats, and writers and artists groups looking for an idyllic venue to host their events.

www.wisteriaacres.com
ww.theunbridledsoul.com
Facebook: Wisteria Acres Wellness & Retreats
LinkedIn: linkedin.com/in/krista-brown-05b94231/
Instagram: @wisteriaacres

CPSIA information can be obtained
at www.ICGtesting.com
Printed in the USA
LVOW10s2018020318
568482LV00012B/886/P